The Bayeux Tapestry is unique, not only
by virtue of its age, but also because
it is an artistic and cultural testimonial
which gives a startling insight into
people's lives in the late Viking Age.
The 70-metre-long tapestry is illustrated
here in its entirety. Each complete
scene, with the text belonging to it,
is reproduced on a double page of the
book – exactly as the artist may have
wished it in his time. The beautiful and
often dramatic pictures are presented
and explained by the Danish archaeo-
logist Mogens Rud. The author provides
background material on contemporary
political and dynastic conflicts; he gives
a vivid account of the living conditions
of the Vikings, who are so realistically
portrayed in the Bayeux Tapestry's
multicoloured embroidery.

MOGENS RUD

The Bayeux Tapestry
is reproduced with
special permission from
the City of Bayeux

The Bayeux Tapestry

AND THE BATTLE OF HASTINGS 1066

Christian Ejlers Publishers · Copenhagen

Mogens Rud
THE BAYEUX TAPESTRY
and the Battle of Hastings, 1066
Copyright © Mogens Rud 1983, 2002

Published in Danish under the title
BayeuxTapetet og slaget ved Hastings 1066

Fifth English edition, first printing 2004

Translated from the Danish by Chris Bojesen
Reproduction: AKA-print, Aarhus, Denmark
Printed by AKA-print, Aarhus, Denmark

ISBN 87 7241 020 5

Danish edition ISBN 87 7241 358 1
French edition ISBN 87 7241 024 8
German edition ISBN 87 7241 022 1
Norwegian edition ISBN 87 7241 026 4
Swedish edition ISBN 87 7241 350 6

Christian Eilers, Publishers
Sølvgade 38/3, DK-1307 Copenhagen K
Fax +45 3312 2884
liber@ce-publishers.dk

The Bayeux Tapestry is exhibited at the
Centre Guillaume le Conquérant
Rue de Nesmond, F 14400 Bayeux, Normandie, France

Contents

Note on the photography
The scale of the reproduction is approximately
14 per cent of the original.

Preface

The Bayeux Tapestry is an embroidered hanging worked in wool on linen. Perhaps the use of these humble materials has enabled this work of art to survive while so much other contemporary handicraft, adorned with pearls and precious stones and worked in gold thread, has perished through warfare and looting. This is a full-scale detail of the dining scene on page 71. Bishop Odo of Bayeux is blessing the food, observed by his half-brother William, Duke of Normandy, later known as William the Conqueror.

Over 900 years have passed since the Bayeux Tapestry was made. It is a unique historical and cultural memento, featuring the series of events in England and Normandy which led up to the invasion by William the Conqueror in 1066, and culminating with the description of the famous Battle of Hastings – or as *The Anglo-Saxon Chronicle* calls it: the 'Battle of the Grey Apple-Tree'.

This book starts with a survey of what the Bayeux Tapestry is: its themes, the technique used to produce it and the history of the tapestry itself. Then there follow some brief chapters outlining the background to the events illustrated, and the chief personages presented: the English King, Edward the Confessor; his successor, Earl Harold Godwinson; William, Duke of Normandy; and his half-brother Odo, Bishop of Bayeux. In the book's central section the entire tapestry is reproduced from original photographs in Bayeux. Each scene is accompanied by a detailed description, often supplemented by evidence from contemporary written sources. The concluding chapter tells what happened immediately after the end of the story narrated in the tapestry, i.e. after the Battle of Hastings, covering the coronation of William I as King of England and his fortunes until his death in 1087.

The book's text is based on both contemporary and more recent sources from England, France and Scandinavia (see bibliography). Where the older sources do not agree, I have kept to the findings of the most recent researchers, the English in particular. In a few cases I have myself ventured to put forward a new interpretation of a controversial feature. Besides recording sober and historically confirmed descriptions and data I have cited a good deal of legendary material which should help reflect a picture of people and incidents which popular tradition has preserved for close on a thousand years.

The now late Francis Wormald, Professor of Palaeography of London University, was so kind as to indicate to me sources for various scenes in the Bayeux Tapestry. I also wish to convey my most cordial thanks to the following: the former conservator of the Bayeux Tapestry over a long period of years, Mademoiselle Simone Bertrand of Bayeux, for having given me the opportunity to study the hangings at close quarters, and for valuable information about its production and history; to the distinguished members of the Battle and District Historical Society, Battle, East Sussex: to the Secretary of the Museum Committee, Miss J. E. S. Robertson, and the Vice-President of the Society, Brigadier-General D. A. Learmont, both of whom very kindly answered questions and guided me round when visiting the battlefield of Hastings; and in addition to the numerous authors, now living and some long-deceased, without whose research and findings I could not have written this book. In my descriptions of persons and events, I have endeavoured to remain impartial. If I have been successful in this, it may perhaps be due to the fact that I am a Dane and as such a kinsman of both the Anglo-Saxons and the Normans.

This is the fifth edition of the *Bayeux Tapestry*. The Tapestry is shown in a, digital reproduction based on photographs lent by the *Centre Guillaume le Conquérant*, Bayeux, where it is displayed. I should like to thank *Mme Liliane Bouillon-Pasquet*, the former Director of the museum, for her interest and help.

Part of the fifth edition (pp 9-37) has been revised; I thank professor Pierre Bouet, Office d'Etudes Normandes, University of Caen, for his critical reading and constructive suggestions.

The Bayeux Tapestry is now available in Danish, English, French, German, Norwegian, and Swedish.

Copenhagen, May 2004   *Mogens Rud*

The embroidery in Bayeux

… a very long and very narrow strip of linen, embroidered with figures and inscriptions representing the Conquest of England, which is hung round the nave of the church on the Feast of relics and throughout the Octave.
Inventory of Notre Dame Cathedral of Bayeux, 1476

TAPISSERIE – *Tapestry* – is what is announced on the signs with arrows guiding the visitors through the lovely old Norman town of Bayeux, and into the Centre Guillaume le Conquérant, the former theological seminary in the Allée des Augustines. Here one of the greatest historical treasures of France is on display to the public.

Despite its name, the Bayeux hanging is not a 'tapestry' in the established sense of the term, i.e. a Gobelin; its images are not woven but embroidered. One might call it the 'Bayeux Embroidery', yet the original meaning of the word 'tapestry' only signified a 'hanging' and, since the traditional designation of this work of art has long been accepted, we shall also use it here.

The Bayeux Tapestry is a pictorial hanging – 'a long and narrow strip of linen' – a little over 70 metres (230 feet) long and about half a metre (20 inches) wide. It is obvious that it once was even longer, because the border running above and below it is intact at the left end, but missing on the right where the material has been torn. There are theories concerning certain concluding scenes, but let us keep those until we get to that stage in the description of the events in the tapestry.

The series of incidents depicted in the Bayeux Tapestry, and recounted in Latin in summary texts on it, took place in England and in the French Duchy of Normandy opposite the south coast of England. They occurred in the years from 1064 to 1066, when Sweyn Estridsen reigned in Denmark and Harold Hardrada in Norway. The main protagonists are the English Earl and later King Harold Godwinson and the Norman Duke William, called 'the Bastard' on account of his illegitimate birth, and later 'the Conqueror' after his conquest of England. Its main theme is William's invasion of England in 1066 with its culmination in the depiction of the Battle of Hastings on 14 October the same year. A third person who appears several times is William's half-brother, Bishop Odo of Bayeux. Modern researchers are of the opinion that it was he who had the tapestry made to adorn his new cathedral.

Various features suggest that the hanging was produced during the first decade after the last incidents it depicts. The cathedral in Bayeux was consecrated in 1077 and it seems reasonable that Bishop Odo would have wished to have the hanging ready for that occasion. In that case, given the scale of the piece of handicraft, work on it must have commenced immediately after the victory at Hastings. This assumption is supported by the fact that the tapestry depicts several events that are incomprehensible today, or seemingly insignificant in comparison with incidents of importance to the whole course of events. They must have been episodes that were common knowledge at an early date, but were then soon forgotten. In reviewing the individual scenes, attention will be drawn to incidents of this type.

In its entire style and technique, the Bayeux Tapestry closely resembles other pictorial productions from the later half of the 11th century; but who was responsible for producing it and where was it made?

In France it is still often called 'Tapisserie de la reine Mathilde' – 'Queen Matilda's tapestry' – because of a tradition (which is however hardly older than about 1800) that it was the wife of William the Conqueror who had had it made in honour of her consort, and had perhaps even worked on its embroidery personally. It is not impossible that she commissioned the work, although in that case she herself would most likely have figured in it. But then why should it have become a permanent fixture in the little town of Bayeux, rather than in the ducal capital of Rouen, or in Caen where Matilda had built a large convent which she afterwards supported? It is quite unlikely that she alone could have produced it. It would have been an insurmountable task for a single person, let alone for a woman in her position with official duties as Queen of England and Duchess of Normandy. That it was embroidered by women is plausible, and the names are known of several women of that time who were renowned for their handicraft, for instance Edith, the wife of Edward the Confessor.

In any case, where was the Bayeux Tapestry produced? Most researchers say in England, and they base their assumption on several facts. There was at that time a renowned school for decorative embroidery in Canterbury, county town of Kent in south-east England (Odo became Earl of Kent after the Conquest). The style and technique of the hanging also points in the direction of that school. Secondly, it has been established that the details of a number of scenes are clearly inspired by illustrations

The artist of the Bayeux Tapestry, despite ignorance of Perspective and with only needle and thread as the medium, has succeeded in creating a series of amazingly vivid scenes, like this one, in which Harold Godwinson and William of Normandy meet for the first time. In the centre is Count Guy of Ponthieu who is pointing out the English Earl to his liege lord. The very different physiognomies of the two principal actors are clearly portrayed. The borders above and below the main frieze in the tapestry are filled in with diverse subjects: animals and birds, mythical creatures, scenes from daily life etc., separated by sloping bars and various small ornaments. Tall buildings and ships' masts reach up in places into the upper border. When describing the great battle, the whole of the lower border is incorporated into the main scene. In this section, two birds and two camels appear above, and a naked couple and two dragons below.

in Anglo-Saxon illuminated manuscripts from the 10th and 11th centuries and that the vivid and stirring character of the many scenes, taken as a whole, bears the stamp of Anglo-Saxon tradition rather than any other. Lastly, linguistic experts have noted that in certain places the Latin inscriptions accompanying the events reveal a way of spelling proper names that seems to be of English origin. Examples of this nature will also be given in due course.

It is likely that the embroidery was made by women, yet at the same time that the designing was done by a man. The detailed representations of military equipment, fiery war-horses and extremely realistic battle scenes dispel any doubt. The entire hanging was presumably designed by one man, for

in spite of the wealth of variety in content, there is a striking homogeneity in the whole pattern of the tapestry.

Stitches, thread and colours

The long strip of linen is made up of nine bands sewn together. It is hardly possible to find any trace of the original drawings in the places where the thread has now disappeared; the whole must originally have been outlined, perhaps on a separate pattern, with nothing left to improvisation.

The embroidery is sewn with two-ply wool yarn; the main stitches used are stem stitch and laid-and-couched work (see illustration on next page). All the outlines and the beautiful inch-high letters of the inscriptions are sewn with stem stitch. Where there is the colour of skin, for instance, the linen is left bare (see the section on page 6).

Today we can distinguish eight colours or shades in the wool used. The five principal colours are terracotta, blue-green, light-green, buff and greyish blue. A darker green, a yellow and a very dark blue, which can almost appear black, are also used. How much the original colours have faded, or have otherwise changed, it is not possible to establish. Despite the unsatisfactory storage and other rough treatment of the Bayeux Tapestry through the centuries and not least thanks to excellent restoration work and display, the colours today remain surprisingly bright and the effect of the whole design is clear and striking.

The colours are largely applied at random or to emphasise a dramatic effect. A horse can be red or blue. A certain plasticity is achieved in the picture, which is otherwise drawn without perspective, for instance by using different colours to depict the outer sides of the two nearer legs of a horse and the inner sides of its two other legs (see illustration on pages 10-11).

Woven or embroidered figured hangings narrating heroic deeds in the sagas, or reproducing wellknown religious subjects, were rather common even in pre-Viking times. Festive halls were decked with hangings, as was already related in the eighth-century saga about Beowulf: 'The gay hanging was worked in gold with Helge's noble deeds …'. At Oseberg in Norway there was a ship burial find from Viking times, about 850 AD, where there were indications that the woman's burial chamber had been hung with figured hangings of which some fragments still remained. German and French narrative hangings from the 11th and 12th centuries are known, but on the whole very few, mostly fragments, have survived.

For edification and instruction

Figured hangings like the Bayeux Tapestry would have been accessible to ordinary people, at any rate on certain occasions; they were thus used in much the same way as medieval frescoes, not only to decorate a church interior, but also, equally important, to tell an edifying story to the many illiterate people of those times. The Bayeux Tapestry also contains a moral: for a man to break his sacred oath is a sin against God – and the wages of sin is death.

The reason the Bayeux Tapestry occupies a quite unique position among pictorial hangings of the period is partly that it is so large and so incredibly well-preserved, and partly that it depicts a series of historical events well-known from literature, which it is able to confirm, and indeed in some cases to supplement. The invaluable significance of the Bayeux Tapestry for cultural history lies, among other things, in its vivid and detailed representation - though often stylised and at times almost naive – of a number of the features of both daily life and warfare which gave shape to human existence at a point in time which can be precisely dated. For Scandinavians these pictures possess special interest in that they show conditions and objects which in many cases correspond closely to those of their own culture during the late Viking age.

Diagrammatic representation of the main forms of stitches used in the Bayeux Tapestry. Top, left-turned stem stitch, used for outlines and lettering. Below, laid-and-couched work, also known as Bayeux stitch, used for filling in areas. In laid-and-couched work the wool is stitched flat over the material within the stem stitch outline; it is then over-stitched at right angles and fastened down with small holding-stitches. In a few places split stitch is used; chain stitch only occurs where the tapestry has later been repaired (see also illustration on page 16).

The cathedral in Bayeux, which was completed and consecrated by Bishop Odo in 1077, enumerated the tapestry among its treasures right up to about the year 1800. In our days the Bayeux Tapestry is placed in the Centre de Guillaume le Conquérant. The Cathedral lies in the centre of the lovely little town which was not damaged during World War II despite the fact that landings took place on the coast at Arromanches less than eight miles away. Photo: M. R.

In its approximately fifty scenes, the Bayeux Tapestry displays a wealth of subjects. A painstaking researcher has counted their components and arrived at the result that the hanging depicts 623 human figures, 202 horses, 55 dogs, 505 other creatures (including birds and fabulous beasts), 37 buildings, 41 ships and boats, 49 trees and nearly 2,000 letters besides. The episodes include, for instance, hunting, ship-building, navigation, cooking and eating, religious ceremonies, battles and the construction of defenceworks. Details illustrated show apparel, riding gear, weapons and other military equipment, reliquaries, etc.

All these items in the Bayeux Tapestry, when viewed as a composite whole hung around the walls of the spacious hall in its home town, make a strong impression on the beholder. Yet before it ended up here in safety and under careful supervision, it had experienced a turbulent history.

A miracle that it exists

Strangely enough the earliest reference to the tapestry is as late as 1476 in the inventory of treasures in the Church of Notre-Dame of Bayeux, which is quoted on page 9 (apart from the indirect reference mentioned on page 88). Its history until then is unknown. However it is quite likely that, in the 400 years that elapsed after its production, it had been preserved in the cathedral for which, as earlier suggested, it had been intended from the beginning.

Nearly 250 years pass before we find another written reference to the Bayeux Tapestry. In 1724 the Académie Royale des Inscriptions et Belles-Lettres received a letter from a Monsieur Lancelot concerning 'a souvenir of William the Conqueror', of which he had obtained a sketch from a friend.

Monsieur Lancelot was in doubt whether it represented 'a bas-relief, a fresco, a glass painting or possibly a tapestry'. He did not receive an answer until several years later when other persons began to be interested in the subject.

Meanwhile a cleric, Dom Bernard de Montfaucon, investigated the matter and discovered that the sketch showed a small portion of a tapestry stored in the cathedral in Bayeux. In 1728 he induced the Prior of Saint-Vigor Monastery in the city to study the whole tapestry and to copy the inscriptions. The following year the first volume of the work *Monuments de la Monarchie francaise* appeared with 14 plates showing the first section of the tapestry.

In 1746 the tapestry was mentioned for the first time in England, in the work *Palaeographia Britannica*.

1792 was a turbulent year for the tapestry, as it was in so many other respects in France under the Revolution. The citizens of Bayeux mustered to fight for the republic. Waggons leaving for the military camps were crowded with men and goods and covered with canvas. There was insufficient cloth for all the vehicles, and some bright person remembered the wonderfully large roll of linen stored in the cathedral! The tapestry was fetched and soon another of the waggons about to depart was covered as satisfactorily as the rest.

Lambert Léonard-Leforestier, lawyer and member of the Bayeux City Council, was the man who saved the tapestry from destruction in 1792. This painting hangs in the museum lobby. Photo: Monsieur Le Monnier.

A few minutes later the Bayeux hanging could have been lost for ever, as has happened to so many national treasures during wars and revolutions. Fortunately, at the last moment one of the members of the local council, a respected lawyer, Monsieur Lambert Léonard-Leforestier, whose name should be gratefully remembered, harangued the mob and succeeded in making them realise what they were doing. He ordered that the tapestry be taken down and replaced with sacking. Then he had the treasure carried into his office to save it from further damage. When the troubles were over Monsieur Léonard-Leforestier returned it to the care of the city council.

Just two years later, however, the Bayeux Tapestry was again in danger. 'On 10 Ventôse, year II' (23 February 1794) the city's newly set up Fine Arts Commission saved it from being cut into pieces to be used as decoration on the occasion of a public holiday! This incident stimulated the Commission to take greater care of the city's treasure. In reply to a rather curt query from the Comité d'Instruction Publique in Paris as to why the tapestry was not listed in the inventories of artistic works which they had been sent, the Bayeux Fine Arts Commission stated boldly that the 'Tapestry of Duke William' was considered to be under the Commission's jurisdiction, which included antiquities. 'The Tapestry has finally been entrusted to our care and we shall now enter it in our inventory.'

For a number of years the hanging was kept under careful supervision by the city council. In 1803, however, on orders from the highest quarters, it was dispatched to Paris under protest. Here, under the designation 'the Tapestry of Queen Matilda', it was displayed in a museum. Napoleon himself showed very special interest in this historic document, representing as it did a successful French invasion of hated England! After abandoning his plan to attempt something similar, Napoleon had the tapestry returned to Bayeux.

Over the following years, the tapestry was moved about several times within the city of Bayeux. It suffered some damage by being placed in a

The tree with interlaced branches – interpreted by some as the 'tree of life' an offshoot of the old Nordic ash Yggdrasil – is the prettiest and most elaborate of the many that serve to separate the various scenes in the tapestry. In the middle stands Count Guy of Ponthieu, whose costume is an example of the most elegant fashion of the times. The artist who designed the tapestry has reproduced details meticulously. In the border below are farming scenes: ploughing with a wheel-plough drawn by a donkey, sowing and harrowing.

contrivance where it could be rolled from one cylinder to another to display a portion at a time.

In 1818 the Society of Antiquaries of London sent a competent draughtsman to Bayeux to make a copy in colour of the entire tapestry. He spent two years on the task and by meticulous study of almost invisible traces of missing threads and of minute needle-holes, he succeeded in creating the basis for a reconstruction of some of the damaged portions.

In 1819 the Danish historian Hector F. J. Estrup, later Director of Sorø Academy, visited the Bayeux Tapestry. In his book *Observations on a journey in Normandy in the autumn of 1819* he states that he had nothing to add to earlier descriptions.

Since the tapestry had suffered from being brought out and shown to prominent visitors, it was suggested time and again that a permanent exhibition under satisfactory conditions should be mounted. It was not until 1842, however, that a display was set up under glass in a room in the city's public library. At the same time some much needed repairs were effected.

At one time during the Franco-Prussian War of 1870-71, when the Prussian forces approached Normandy, the tapestry was taken down and placed in a zinc container, but as soon as the danger had passed, it was again put on display.

In 1913 it was moved to a more suitable building where it remained until the outbreak of World War II in September 1939, when it was placed in an air-raid shelter. During the German occupation of France, the occupying forces demanded on several occasions to see the tapestry. It was exhibited as in the old days by rolling it from one cylinder to another. Once again an enemy of England had sought inspiration for an invasion across the sea, but also this time the opportunity was missed.

However, in 1944 an invasion succeeded in the opposite direction. On D-day, 6 June, several thousand ships and landing craft put out from British ports across the Channel for the coast of Normandy. To avoid destruction during the impending military action, the Bayeux Tapestry was hastily dispatched to Paris and safely deposited in a cellar of the Louvre. When the capital was liberated, the tapestry was exhibited to the public in the closing months of 1944.

After the end of the war in 1945, the hanging returned to its home town and, on the fourth anniversary of the Allied landings, the inauguration of the new exhibition gallery took place in the presence of the President of the French Republic, Monsieur Vincent Auriol.

The Bayeux Tapestry is now in the custody of the Bayeux Municipal Library.

A strip cartoon of its time

And now, returning to the museum, we find a large room with dimmed lighting where show-cases contain what has been called, in the fashion of our time, 'the oldest strip cartoon in the world'. There is some justification for the description. The Bayeux Tapestry contains all the ingredients demanded of a good comic strip: excitement, romance, treachery and conflict. It is only rather short of women, apart from two appearances in the pictorial frieze of a little naked figure, only three women are depicted: Edward the Confessor's Queen Edith, a mysterious

Early in the nineteenth century a little piece of the tapestry disappeared. The wife of Charles Stothard, the English artist who was preparing drawings of the tapestry, has been blamed for this loss, but without any foundation. The fragment, coming from the upper border, turned up later at a London auction. It was acquired by the Victoria and Albert Museum, which in 1871 obligingly delivered it to Bayeux. The damage had in the meantime been repaired and the fragment is now in the custody of the keeper of the tapestry. It is shown here from both sides in full-scale, and the embroidery technique, particularly the 'laid-and-couched work' is clearly manifested. Photo: Zodiaque.

girl called Ælfgyva and an anonymous English woman fleeing from a burning house. Moreover, the figures here are not supplied with exclamations in balloons (no 'SIGH' for the queen at the bedside of the dying king, no 'AAHH!' of awesome admiration at the sight of the comet, no 'UGH!' 'WHAM!' or 'GROAN' from the battling or wounded warriors). There are only terse explanations, soberly located above the scenes, in the international language of the time, Latin.

Today electronic equipment helps to supplement the information provided in this moribund language. The visitor walks past the long series of picturesque and dramatic episodes, with rented earphones, to hear an exhaustive commentary, in the major language of his choice, on what is happening in the scene before him.

Later we shall likewise let the pictures pass in review with an accompanying text. However, to give the reader a complete understanding of the persons observed and of the events taking place, we shall first briefly introduce the chief actors and relate something of their history up to the moment when the narrative starts in the Bayeux Tapestry.

It is as if the designer of the tapestry was not interested in the women behind the great men in the drama. Queen Edith is portrayed here as a distinctly subordinate character. Her features are scarcely delineated and yet the artist has managed to present an excellent picture of a sorrowing woman in her mourning veil. The inscription says: 'Here King Edward is talking to his faithful. And here he expired.' The inscription uses a rounded or squared letter 'E' at random.

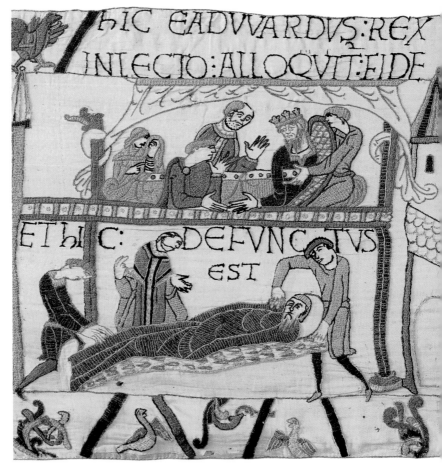

The King, Earls, Duke and Bishop

In many and various ways this was a most disastrous year: the weather was severe and the crops suffered; during this same year more cattle died than anyone remembered before…

The Anglo-Saxon Chronicle, 1042

The wedding feast
beside the Thames

On 8 June 1042 a magnificent wedding was held on a Danish farm in Lambeth beside the Thames near London. The Danish thane Osgod Klapa's daughter Gyda was being married to the royal courtier Tovi Prude. At the height of the festivities, Hardicanute, King of England and Denmark, rose to toast the bride. At that very moment he suffered a stroke and collapsed in a spasm. Those nearest caught him as he fell. The young king, son of Canute the Great, had lost the power of speech. He was borne away and died a few days later.

This dramatic event, which abruptly broke up a Danish wedding party in England, meant at the same time the end of 28 years of Danish rule in England. Hardicanute had died childless, but he had already nominated his successor to the throne of England. It was not to be his Danish cousin Sweyn Estridsen, who might perhaps have continued the Danish dynasty for some time; instead it was his English stepbrother Edward (later called 'the Confessor'), son of his mother's first marriage to Ethelred the Unready, King of England (see genealogical table on page 100). Guided as it were by a premonition of his early demise – he only attained the age of 24 – Hardicanute had had Edward called to his court less than a year before, and had begun to prepare him for kingship.

The mother of Hardicanute and Edward was called Emma. She was the daughter of Duke Richard I of Normandy and his beautiful and gifted Danish-Norman mistress and later wife, Gunnor. Emma, called by a contemporary poet the 'Jewel of Normandy', had been given in marriage by her brother Duke Richard II to King Ethelred in 1002, and had then received the Anglo-Saxon name Ælfgifu. It was a union with political motives, and the marriage was never a happy one. A British writer (George Slocombe) has described Ethelred as 'one of the least admirable kings in English history. Weak, capricious, handsome, elegant and vicious'. Ethelred, in the same year that he married Emma ordered the massacre of Danish settlers all over England on St. Brice's Day, 13 November. This atrocity was revenged later by the Danish King Sweyn Forkbeard in a series of bloody raids and the extortion of enormous amounts of Danegeld.

Emma detested her husband and for that reason had no love either for their two sons: Edward and Alfred. When Ethelred was finally defeated in 1013, the Queen fled with her sons to her relations in Normandy. The following year Sweyn Forkbeard died, and his son Canute (the Great) succeeded him in Denmark, later also becoming King of England. In 1017, when this young decisive warrior and astute statesman was about 20 years old, he had Emma, meanwhile widowed, recalled to England. He married her although she was 15 years his senior. She made it a condition for her marriage to Canute that only their joint issue might inherit the throne of England – under no circumstances could Ethelred's children succeed to the throne!

In 1018 Hardicanute was born. As a little boy he was sent to Denmark where his guardian was Ulf Jarl, husband of his paternal aunt Estrid. Canute the Great, before he died in 1035, had Hardicanute made King of Denmark. However, presumably on account of a constant threat to the country from Magnus the Good in Norway, it was

William the Conqueror's greataunt, Queen Emma, daughter of Duke Richard I of Normandy and Gunnor, daughter of a Danish thane, is seen here with her two sons, Hardicanute by Canute the Great, and Edward (the Confessor) by Ethelred the Unready. In the foreground a French monk is presenting the Queen with his manuscript from 1040, known as Emmas eulogy from which this picture originates. Emma was at that time Queen Dowager, having survived both her royal husbands. In the same year Hardicanute became King, only to be succeeded two years later by his half-brother Edward. British Museum.

nearly five years after his father's death before Hardicanute was able to return to England. In the meantime the country was ruled by Harold Harefoot son of Canute and Ælfgifu (a not unusual name those days) also called Alfifa, the daughter of an Anglo-Saxon thane. When this half-brother died in 1040, Hardicanute was chosen as King of England. His brief reign was not a glorious one. Not many tears were shed over his early death, following the wedding party, in 1042, when fate had in diverse ways played such havoc with the isle of Albion.

The King, who lived 'like a monk'

… Danes ruled over this dear land of England for twenty-eight years all told, squandering its riches.
In time he succeeded; noble in armour, a king of excellent virtues, pure and benign, Edward the noble protected his fatherland, his realm and people; until suddenly came that bitter death, which took so cruelly the prince from the earth…

The Anglo-Saxon Chronicle, 1066

Emma, who would have sooner seen a Nordic prince on the throne of England than one of Ethelred's sons, tried to advocate the cause of Magnus the Good, King of Norway and now also of Denmark. However, the choice already made by Hardicanute was binding and 'before he was buried (in Winchester with King Canute, his father) the whole nation chose Edward to be King…' relates the Chronicle.

Edward had lived in Normandy since the defeat of his father, Ethelred, when Edward was only 10 years old. Now, at the age of about 40, he was far more French than English. He preferred to speak French and he was in every way influenced by French culture and tradition. He surrounded himself with French advisors and favoured French prelates: for instance, Prior Robert from the monastery of St. Ouen near Rouen was soon appointed Bishop of London and later Archbishop of Canterbury. He had Dover Castle manned by Norman troops. Much of this was contrary to previous agreements and for the English was a bitter foretaste of the Norman rule which Edward's half-cousin, Duke William – one of the chief characters in this book – would later impose after his conquest of the country.

Shortly after his coronation, Edward repaid his mother for her lack of affection for him. He had all the land owned by Emma appropriated for his own use and, according to the Chronicle, confiscated from her '…an indescribable number of things of gold and silver, because she had been too tightfisted with him'. The priest Stigand, who had just been made bishop, was removed from office and all his property was seized by the King, 'because he (Stigand) was his mother's closest confidant, and she, as was supposed, followed his advice'. He was later rehabilitated.

While Magnus the Good ruled over both Norway and Denmark, Snorre Sturlasson recounts in the *Saga of Magnus the Good* that he dispatched envoys to King Edward in England with a letter in which he invoked an agreement with Hardicanute that if either of them died without leaving sons, the survivor would inherit the realm and people of the other. The letter concluded: 'I demand that you hand over to me the realm, for otherwise I shall come over myself with my Danish and Norwegian forces. He who fortune will favour with victory, must rule over the countries.'

According to the saga, Edward in his answer first carefully traced the inheritance of the kingship from the death of Ethelred to his own election as King. He then continued: 'During all the time that I did not bear the name of king, I served my superiors with the same unassuming fidelity as any of the men not of royal birth. But now I have been crowned and anointed king with the same rights as my father before me, and I do not intend to give up my kingship as long as I live. If King Magnus comes here with his army, I shall meet force with force. He will be free to subjugate England after he has taken my life. Tell him this from me.'

They went back and told King Magnus all they

had been enjoined. The saga concludes thus: 'The king remained silent for a while, then said slowly: "I think it will be most just – and wisest for me – to let King Edward have his country in peace – and so myself cling tightly to the realms God has granted me".'

This mildness showed quite a different attitude from that adopted by both claimant and defendant some years later. When William of Normandy demanded the throne of England from the country's new and resolute King, Harold Godwinson, of whom we shall hear later, the latter rejected the claim. However, William won his demands.

Edward the Confessor, who gained so fine a posthumous reputation, was more interested in religion than in politics throughout his long reign of 24 years. His piety was extolled by contemporary historians. He once vowed to make a pilgrimage to the Holy Land, and in his old age he realised that it would be impossible to fulfil this pledge. He confessed this to the Pope as a sin, and was enjoined as penance to erect a church – the Church of St. Peter the Apostle on Thorney Island to the west of London, the present Westminster Abbey. His piety even went so far that in his marriage he 'lived like a monk' and his legendary chastity resulted also in his dying without issue. Only nine days after his new church was consecrated, he himself was buried behind the high altar. This was on 6 January in the fateful year 1066.

King Edward, later called 'the Confessor' , 1042 – 1066, was the son of an Anglo-Saxon father and a Norman mother.
His youth, spent in exile in Normandy, came to leave its stamp upon his reign.
Silver penny, twice natural size.

Earl Godwin and his children

Godwin had risen to such great eminence as if he ruled the king and all England; his sons were earls and favourites of the king, and his daughter was the king's wedded wife.

The Anglo-Saxon Chronicle, 1052

Edward the Confessor's wife Edith was the daughter of the mighty Earl Godwin of Wessex and sister of another of the chief characters in this narrative: Harold Godwinson, godson of the King, and his favourite.

Early in the 11th century Godwin, who must have been born in about 980, had become one of the leading men in England. He was an Anglo-Saxon of lowly aristocratic descent but had throughout an eventful life attained a position of power in the country 'as if he ruled the King'. This had been attained as a result of his forceful and resolute character, tireless energy and not least his marriage to Gyda, sister to Canute the Great's brother-in-law and deputy in Denmark, Ulf Jarl. Godwin had been Canute's most trusted man in England. After the King's death he had sided with Hardicanute and supported Emma in her resistance to her stepson Harold Harefoot. As time went on, however, and Hardicanute, staying in Denmark, failed to assert his rights in England, both Godwin and Emma were reconciled with King Harold.

In 1036 a violent episode occurred which aroused consternation in many quarters in England. It is reported that Emma wrote to her two sons (by Ethelred), Alfred and Edward, in Normandy saying that the English wanted to make one of them king. Alfred, the younger one, immediately crossed the Channel accompanied by 600 Norman warriors. Soon after he had landed in Dover, he was met by Earl Godwin who gave him a good reception. However, for some inexplicable reason – perhaps a resurgence of his old loyalty to Hardicanute – Godwin shortly afterwards betrayed Alfred to Harold Harefoot's forces. The contemporary Norman historian Guillaume de Poitiers recounts that Prince Alfred was taken prisoner and that nine out of ten of his following were beheaded in his presence. At a Danish court in Ely – where Canute the Great had once enjoyed the chanting of the monks, as an Anglo-Saxon writer records – Alfred was charged with disturbing the peace of the country, found guilty and condemned to be blinded. He did not survive the maltreatment connected with this barbaric punishment.

It is not known with any certainty what role Emma played in this sinister drama, which 30 years later was used to help justify William's conquest of England. However, it is a fact that she was shortly afterwards exiled from England by Harold Harefoot. This time she did not sail across to her relatives in Rouen, but to Flanders, to the gentle Count Balduin V in Bruges, yet another vassal of the French King. From here she implored her son Hardicanute in Denmark to avenge his half-brother's monstrous murder, which she claimed was due to Harold Harefoot and Godwin. However, King Harold died in the spring of 1040. When Hardicanute soon after put into Bruges with 62 longships, he took his mother back to England with him.

Immediately after his arrival there he had his half-brother Harold's body exhumed, beheaded and thrown into the Thames. Thereafter he ordered that Godwin be tried in court. The Earl swore his innocence as regards Alfred's death, with a number of thanes to bear him witness. According to Anglo-Saxon custom, he accompanied his plea of not guilty with a present to the King, a magnificent gift which clearly manifested his wealth. It was a dragon ship ornamented with gilded fittings and manned by 80 fighting men, each with a golden helmet, a gold axe on his left shoulder and a spear in his right hand. Heavy gold armlets were on every arm. Godwin was acquitted.

When Edward came to the throne, Godwin on many occasions was at odds with him. He was bitterly opposed to King Edward's Norman leanings, and after a particularly violent clash, matters went so far that the Earl's and the King's armies prepared for battle. Since neither party in reality wanted open war, the danger was averted, but Godwin had to leave the country. This was in 1051. With his wife Gyda and three of their sons, Sweyn, Tostig and Gyrth, he sailed for Flanders to

Edward the Confessor never overcame his suspicion that Godwin was implicated in the dastardly murder of his brother Alfred. In this miniature from the 13th century, Edward once more accuses the Earl. It is related that at a royal banquet Godwin wished to prove his innocence before the King by swallowing a large piece of meat. However, it stuck fast in his throat and he died...
Public Record Office, Crown copyright, by permission of the Controller of H. M. Stationery Office.

seek asylum with the hospitable Count Balduin, who shortly before had become Tostig's father-in-law. Harold Godwinson and his younger brother Leofwin crossed over to Ireland. Queen Edith, their sister, also incurred the King's disfavour and was sent by him to a convent.

Tostig's wife was called Judith. She had a niece named Matilda who, about this time, became engaged to William, the young Duke of Normandy. The connections between the families intertwine like threads in an intricate pattern (see genealogical table on page 100).

Godwin stayed in Flanders for about a year, from September 1051 to September 1052. Perhaps his absence from England at this time was more fateful for the future of his country than either he or his son Harold could have imagined. Whether by chance or calculation, it would seem that Duke William took advantage of this very period to visit England and Edward the Confessor. During the visit the pro-Norman King promised him the crown of England, as William subsequently maintained, but more about this later.

When Godwin returned to England, he demonstrated in convincing fashion his mastery of the use of both force and diplomacy to recapture his lost position. He assembled a fleet, joined his son Harold who had also mustered one, and successfully sought the support of seamen – Danish among others – in the ports of Kent and Sussex. They sailed up the Thames to London in warlike formation and anchored at Southwark on the south bank. The King's far inferior fleet lay moored opposite them by the north bank. With a daring manoeuvre Godwin then shut in Edward's ships and sent a messenger to the King with a demand for negotiations.

Under these circumstances the King gave way. Bishop Stigand of Winchester, himself a calculating and astute negotiator, led the royal delegation. Civil war between King and Earl was thus averted for a second time in their strained relationship. By this time, some of the King's closest Norman advisers and favourites, among them the hated Archbishop Robert of Canterbury, had fled posthaste out of the country.

Edward the Confessor was a weak King whose posthumous reputation was largely due to his devoted solicitude for the church. The tradition concerning his platonic relationship with his wife Edith, daughter of Earl Godwin, is based on references such as in Vita Edwardi Regis: 'The excellent Queen served him like a daughter' and 'But she kept the secret of the King's chastity which she had experienced...' This picture, a part of the Bayeux Tapestry, shows the King shortly before he died. His full beard indicates that he did not follow the fashion of the time of being clean-shaven or only wearing a moustache. The spiked stick emphasises his frailty. In 1161 King Edward was canonised.

At an assembly at which the 'earls and all the best men of the land' were to pass judgement in the case, Godwin again showed that he knew exactly how to deal with the King. After having cowed him with the threat of force, Godwin pacified him with theatrical humility. The Earl knelt before his King and laid his long battle-axe symbolically at the royal feet. Then he asked permission to plead his case and clear himself of all accusations, new and old. This granted, he made a masterly speech convincing all present – his supporters were in the majority anyway – of his innocence in respect of all charges, among them of complicity in Alfred's death and of desire to put himself above the king.

King Edward, doubtless weak but not stupid, apparently allowed himself to be convinced also, and reinstated Godwin to his former dignity as Earl of Wessex. Godwin's daughter, Queen Edith, was restored to favour.

Earl Harold – 'the boldest man in England'

Six months later, Godwin died after dining with the King, leaving all Wessex (i.e. the whole of southern England from Land's End to Kent) to his son Harold. In 1057 Leofric, Earl of Mercia and East Anglia, died. His earldoms were divided between his son Alfgar who received Mercia, and Harold's brother Gyrth who was given East Anglia. At the same time, Harold himself annexed Herefordshire alongside the border to south Wales. His other brother Leofwine had an earldom created for him, centred on London and embracing south-east England. His third brother Tostig had already received Northumbria in 1055. When Alfgar died in 1062, Mercia went to his young son Edwin who soon came under the influence of his neighbour, Earl Harold.

As head of the powerful house of Godwin, Harold was now incontestably the strong man of the country and in the ailing King Edward's last year he was in practice the regent of England. It was at this time that a chronicler described Harold as being a 'vassal king' – *sub-regulus*.

The tall fair Earl with the charming personality had not won the heart of the King alone; he was widely beloved and admired. The chronicler of *Vita Edwardi Regis* expressed it thus: 'So say the Englishmen that Harold Godwinson has been the boldest man found in England; and that he was the best knight, both of old and new times.'

For a great number of years Harold had a mistress *more danico* (according to Danish custom), the beautiful Edith, nick-named Swan-neck. He had at least three children with her. We hear about two sons who some years after their father's defeat launched an unsuccessful assault on their Norman-occupied homeland (page 93). Saxo in his *Gesta Danorum* gives a short account of the events in England in 1066. He says among other things that after the Battle of Hastings, two sons of Harold and their sister crossed over to Denmark. Here the King, Sweyn Estridsen, received them kindly, as close relatives. Harold's daughter Gyda was given in marriage by King Sweyn to the Grand Duke Vladimir Monomakh, a nephew of Harold Hardrada (King of Norway), the man her father had killed at Stamford Bridge (see page 27). In time Gyda was to become great-grandmother of the Danish King Valdemar the Great (see genealogical table on page 100).

Harold Godwinson's parents, Earl Godwin Wulfnotson and Gyda Torgilsdatter Spragalag, as the saga calls his mother, had nine children in all. The sons were Sweyn, Harold, Tostig, Gyrth, Leofwine and Wulfnoth, the daughters Edith, Gunhild and Ælfgifu (yet another of this popular name!). The elder children's names are Nordic, while the younger ones are definitely Anglo-Saxon.

The eldest son Sweyn, who was Earl of the South-West Midlands, disgraced himself when, on his way home from a raid in Wales in 1046, he seduced the abbess in Leominster. He had to leave the country to spend some years in Denmark. On his return he brought himself into even worse repute. In an attempt to regain his confiscated property, he contrived to have his cousin Earl Beorn (Bjørn), a brother of Sweyn Estridsen, murdered. He was again banished, and this time he went to stay with the ever hospitable Count Balduin in Flanders. From there he travelled on foot on a pilgrimage to Jerusalem, and died in Constantinople on his way home. This was in 1052, at the same time that his father and brother were restored to favour in England.

We do not know very much about the sisters,

apart from Edith, who was Edward the Confessor's allegedly chaste consort. She died in 1075 'and the King (William the Conqueror) had her body brought to Westminster with great ceremony, and buried her beside King Edward, her lord' (*Anglo-Saxon Chronicle*). Queen Edith is one of the few female characters to appear in the Bayeux Tapestry, in fact among the persons about King Edward's deathbed (page 17). The youngest sister, Ælfgifu, was promised by Harold to a Norman baron during the negotiations with William in Normandy in 1065.

Harold's youngest brother Wulfnoth and a young nephew Hakon were given as hostages to the Duke by King Edward presumably in 1052 in connection with his promise to William of the crown of England. This was customary in those days as a pledge of good faith. Three others of Harold's brothers each met, as he did himself, a sudden and violent death. Leofwine and Gyrth died with Harold at Hastings. Tostig was killed only nineteen days before while fighting on the side of King Hardrada of Norway against his own brother, King Harold.

Prior to that, Tostig had been one of the chief actors in a series of significant events.

The Earl of Northumbria, the Dane Siward, had died shortly after having defeated his neighbour to the north, King Macbeth of Scotland. In 1055 King Edward appointed Tostig as his successor, and in the following years Tostig established friendly relations with Malcolm, the new King of Scotland. However, among his own people with their strong element of Danish stock, Tostig never gained the support and confidence that his predecessor had enjoyed. Much of his time was spent away from his earldom, either hunting or on military expeditions. For instance, he helped his brother Harold to defeat the Welsh King Gruffydd who had been ravaging across the border into Herefordshire. Gruffydd was murdered by one of his own men. Later when Harold became King, he abandoned his mistress of many years, Edith Swan-neck, and married Gruffydd's widow, Aldgyth, for political reasons. She was the daughter of Earl

Map of English earldoms in 1066 when Harold Godwinson and his younger brothers owned the largest areas in the country. According to E. A. Freeman.

Alfgar, sister of Earl Edwin of Mercia and his brother Morcar, and grand-daughter of the famous Lady Godiva (who rode naked through Coventry, but that is another story).

In the autumn of 1063, while Tostig was hunting in the south of England together with King Edward, two hundred major farm-owners rose against him, occupied his capital, York, killing any they could of his faithful following, both English and Danish, and emptied his armoury. Then they made Morcar Earl in place of Tostig. With an army reinforced with contingents from Mercia and the Welsh border country, Morcar advanced southward through England. When Tostig did not appear to react to this move against him, the King ordered Harold to send an army against the insurgents. Level-headed Harold advised against resorting to force and obtained the King's permission to try to negotiate with the rebels. While their main forces were ravaging and pillaging just to the north, Morcar and his allies met Harold in Oxford. Here he urged them to lay down their arms and have the case brought before a Witenagemot – an assembly of the Witan, the thanes of the realm. This was rejected and Harold chose to avoid a bloody civil war by advising the King to recognise Morcar as Earl of Northumbria and to banish Tostig. This politically wise move naturally infuriated Tostig who at the meeting accused his brother of supporting the uprising in Northumbria. However, the King and the Witan accepted Harold's proposal and ordered him to make peace with the rebels on their conditions.

Tostig, with his wife and children, went to Flanders to stay for the winter with his brother-in-law, Count Balduin. This settlement, which had certainly pacified Tostig's opponents, had at the same time caused an irremedial rupture between the two brothers. The deposed Earl used his time in Flanders to intrigue against Harold, first in vain with his gentle brother-in-law and then with great success with the most famous and feared warrior of those times, Harold Sigurdsson, King of Norway, known as Hardrada.

Before we hear about Tostig again, Harold God-winson had been in Normandy for a lengthy stay at the court of Duke William. After Harold's return, Edward the Confessor died and Harold himself was chosen King. However, these very events open the narrative in the Bayeux Tapestry and we shall re-serve them for more detailed treatment in the next chapter. Here we shall conclude the account of Tostig and his bitter hatred of Harold by describing Tostig's treachery and the bloody Battle of Stamford Bridge. This event is not depicted in the Bayeux Tapestry, but took place just before William's invasion, and was a contributing factor in the fatal defeat of the English at the Battle of Hastings.

The Battle of Stamford Bridge

The Anglo-Saxon Chronicle gives a concise and realistic report of what happened in an almost modern journalistic form:

"Then while the ships were in port, King Harold from Norway came unexpectedly north into the Tyne with a great pirate host – it was anything but small, for it numbered about three hundred ships or more – and Earl Tostig joined him, as they had previously agreed, with all the host he had been able to muster. They sailed together with their combined troops along the Ouse up towards York. King Harold, to the south, was informed when he came ashore that King Harold of Norway and Earl Tostig had landed near York. Thereupon he marched northward, day and night, as quickly as he could assemble his levies; but before King Harold could arrive, Earl Edwin and Earl Morcar had gathered as great a force as they could from their earldom, and fought that host and made great slaughter of them; but a great number of the English were either slain or drowned or driven in flight, and the Norwegians had possession of the place of slaughter. This battle took place on the vigil of St. Matthew the Apostle (20 September) which was a Wednesday. After the battle King Harold of Norway and Earl Tostig entered York with as great a force as seemed to them necessary and received hostages from the borough, besides assistance in the way of provisions, and so retired thence to their ships. They offered to conclude an abiding peace with the citizens provided that they all marched southward with them to conquer this realm. Then meanwhile came Harold, the King of the English, with all his levies on the Sunday to Tadcaster and there drew up his household troops in battle order; and on the Monday he marched through York. Harold, King of Norway, and Earl Tostig and their force had gone from their ships beyond York to Stamford Bridge, for it had been expressly promised them that hostages would be brought to meet them there from the whole of the shire. Their Harold, King of the English, came upon them unawares beyond the bridge. They joined battle and fierce fighting went on until late in the day; and there Harold, King of Norway, was slain and Earl Tostig and countless numbers of men with them, both English and Norwegians".

Snorre describes in *Harold Hardrada's Saga* an epi-sode occurring just before the battle commenced. The two armies were facing one another when:

"Twenty horsemen from the English King's company of Housecarls came riding up to the Norwegian lines; they were all wearing coats of mail, and so were their horses.

One of the riders said, 'Is Earl Tostig here in this army?'

Tostig replied, 'There is no denying it – you can find him here.'

Another of the riders said, 'Your brother King Harold sends you his greetings and this message to say you can have peace and the whole of Northumbria as well. Rather than have you refuse to join him, he is prepared to give you one third of all his kingdom.'

The Earl answered, 'This is very different from all the hostility and humiliation he offered me last winter. If this offer had been made then, many a man who is now dead would still be alive, and England would now be in better state. But if I accept this offer now, what will he offer King Harold Sigurdsson for all his effort?'

The rider said, 'King Harold has already declared how much of England he is prepared to grant him: seven feet of ground, or as much as he is taller than men.'

Earl Tostig said, 'Go now and tell King Harold to make ready for battle. The Norwegians will never be able to say that Earl Tostig abandoned King Harold Sigurdsson to join his enemies when he came west to fight in England. We are united in our aim: Either to die with honour, or else conquer England.'

The horseman now rode back.

Then King Harold Sigurdsson asked, 'Who was that man who spoke so well?'

'That was King Harold Godwinson,' replied Tostig.

King Harold Sigurdsson said, 'I should have been told much sooner. These men came so close to our lines that this Harold should not have lived to tell of the deaths of our men.'

'It is quite true, sire,' said Earl Tostig, 'that the King acted unwarily, and what you say could well have happened. But I realised that he wanted to offer me my life and great dominions, and I would have been his murderer if I revealed his

'This Harold was the richest of all the King's subjects and supreme in honour and power' relates the contemporary writer Guillaume de Poitiers. The tall, well-built, Nordic-blond Earl, second son of Godwin and thus brother-in-law of King Edward, is seen here in the Bayeux Tapestry being offered the crown of England. In 1066 Harold Godwinson did not deny that he had offered Duke William the crown on behalf of the King, but since Edward on his deathbed had entrusted his country to the popular Earl, and since the people of England themselves had confirmed this choice, Harold felt released from his promise to William. Harold was then about 44 years old and in the same year he was killed at the Battle of Hastings.

identity. I would rather that he were my killer than I his.'

King Harold Sigurdsson said to his men, 'What a little man that was, but he stood proudly in his stirrups.'

The battle was fierce and bloody, but it was not until Harold Hardrada's emblem, the famous

'Land-Waster' banner had changed its bearer three times, their King himself had been killed by an arrow piercing his throat and Tostig had also fallen, that the Norwegians gave in. The English-born Norman historian, the monk Orderic Vital, recounted half a century afterwards that the battlefield was still, so much later, 'easily recognisable by the heaps of skeletons witnessing to this day to the heavy losses of both peoples'.

The following days were spent by the victor of Stamford Bridge in York, where he buried his dead brother and negotiated with those Norwegian leaders who had survived. He made them promise never to attack England again and let them go home in peace. Twenty-four of the three hundred ships that had come from Norway were able to carry all the survivors.

Although triumphant and full of pride, the English army was also greatly weakened. Few imagined that at that very moment another enemy had embarked, prepared for war and firmly resolved to conquer England. Harold was still in York when on 1 October a thane from Pevensey on the Channel coast was announced. He had ridden for three days and nights when, exhausted and mud-spattered, he sought audience with the King. His message was what Harold had anticipated and feared: William the Bastard had landed with an army of Norman horsemen…

William the Bastard, Duke of Normandy

Harold has wronged me in taking the Kingdom which was granted and promised to me, as he himself has sworn. …If God please I will seek my right.

Duke William in Wace's Roman de Rou

It is recounted that when William, the son of Duke Robert of Hièsmois, was born in 1027 or 1028 in the Castle of Falaise in the heart of Normandy, he was laid on a heap of oat straw, which in those days was strewn on cold earthen or stone floors for warmth. The boy at once began to reach for and grasp hold of the straw, soon collecting an armful. The women gathered round the newborn infant took this as a good omen; the young lord is starting early 'to accumulate and take possession'.

It was nothing unusual that Robert's son was a 'bastard'. The same was the case with his grandfather, great-grandfather and great-great-grandfather. The old dukes had all been illegitimate children (see genealogical table on page 102). Yet times had changed and moral codes had not become more liberal. On the contrary, the Church condemned to a greater degree than it did earlier any liaisons entered into without its blessing.

Duke Robert himself used the term 'bastard' about his 7- or 8-year-old son when taking leave of his barons and courtiers to do penance by making a pilgrimage to Jerusalem. 'Believe me, it is not of my own will that I leave you without a lord. I have here a little bastard, who with God's help will grow up and become a brave man. Therefore

'In this year King Edward passed away, and Earl Harold came to the throne and ruled for forty weeks and a day', relates the Anglo-Saxon Cronicle. Though Harold Godwinson's reign was so short, he yet managed to have coins struck with his portrait, like this silver penny minted in London during his single year on the throne, 1066 (three times enlarged).

I enjoin you, by the duty you owe me, to receive him as your lord. That he was born out of wedlock means very little to you; he will be no less fitted for warfare or for dispensing justice.' (The name, William the Bastard, was used mostly by his opponents. Yet one instance is known, at any rate, when many years later he himself signed his name as *Villelmus Nothus*, William the Bastard.)

The assembly of nobles then demonstrated their recognition of their new lord by coming forward one by one, and clasping his boyish hands in their palms, swearing allegiance to him. Robert thereupon placed his son under the protection of his cousin, Alain of Brittany, and of his overlord, King Henry I of France. He chose Gilbert of Brionne to be his guardian; as his grand seneschal or majordomo his cousin Osbern, a son of the dowager Duchess Gunnor the Dane's brother Herfast; and as his tutor Thurold. These were all tried and loyal henchmen.

A journey to the Holy Land was a lengthy and risky venture, and though the Duke was only 25 years of age, he foresaw that he might not return home alive. Therefore he finally addressed one of his most faithful knights, the young Count Herluin of Conteville, and enjoined him to marry William's mother, Herleva, should he die during his travels.

Herleva, or Arletta as she became nicknamed, was the daughter of Fulbert, a tanner in Falaise. (Many years later, the citizens in a town besieged by William made fun of his descent by hanging out hides over the city walls, and the Bastard took frightful revenge upon them in his fury.)

According to popular tradition in Normandy the liaison between Robert and Arletta arose in this way: One day in the spring of 1027, when Arletta was not quite 17 years old, she was washing clothes in a little river flowing past the castle in Falaise, when Count Robert rode by on his way home from falconry. He himself was not much older than her, but old enough to fall passionately in love with the beautiful girl. Soon after this first meeting, Robert sent a message to the tanner's daughter asking her to come to him at the castle

discreetly at night. Arletta was indeed of the common people and would hardly be unaffected by the dashing young Count's attention, but she was not the sort who would guiltily sneak to a rendezvous under cover of darkness. Oh no, if the Count wished to see her, she would come in style; in full daylight, mounted on a steed; the drawbridge lowered in her honour and an appropriate suite prepared for her. Robert must have respected her attitude, for he gave in to her wishes. Within a year a little boy was born, to be given the name of William. When Robert's elder brother, Duke Richard III, died, and Robert inherited the title, he and Arletta moved with their little son to the ducal court in Rouen.

Descendant of the Viking

William was the sixth generation of the Norman ducal family. His great-great-great-grandfather was the mighty Viking chieftain Rollo, or Rou as the medieval writer Robert Wace calls him, or Ganger-Rolf, son of Ragnvald, Earl of More, as he appears in the Nordic saga. On concluding peace with the French King Charles the Simple in the year 911, Rollo was baptised and given the name of Robert. At the same time, he was made Count of the part of northern France which is still known as Normandy. Like the hero in the fairy tale, Rollo won both 'half the kingdom' and the hand of the princess. The French king bestowed his daughter Gisèle upon his new vassal, whose principal task was to protect his realm against future Viking raids. After the death of the princess some years later, Rollo renewed his relationship with his former mistress Poppa, whose father, Count Beranger of Bayeux, he had killed in battle. Poppa became mother to Duke William I, called Longsword, whose son Duke Richard I, the Fearless, again married a French princess. However, all his children were by his beautiful and wise mistress Gunnor, 'who came from a very noble Danish family', as Guillaume de Jumieges writes in his Norman history. When the princess died, he married the Danish girl.

Richard's encounter with Gunnor, according to legend, had a piquancy worthy of a French film. While hunting in his extensive forests, the young Duke and his followers were overtaken by nightfall and they sought lodgings for the night with one of his foresters. The Duke immediately fell in love with the forester's beautiful young wife. The spouse had already resigned himself to the traditional right of his liege lord to the conjugal bed, when his faithful wife sent her sister Gunnor, likewise young and beautiful, but unmarried, to the Duke's bed-chamber in her stead. Apparently the trick worked out to the satisfaction of all parties.

Gunnor bore Richard the Fearless at least four children. She saw her son become Duke of Normandy as Richard II, the Good. Her daughter Emma (see page 18) first married King Ethelred the Unready and next Canute the Great. Two grandsons, Dukes Richard III and Robert I, the Magnificent (William's father), succeeded one after the other to the dukedom. She was still living when her great-grandson William was born in the castle in Falaise.

Gunnor's son Duke Richard II also became re-lated to the Danish royal house in another way besides his sister Emma's marriage to Canute the Great. It appears that after the death of his first wife, he married King Canute's sister Estrid, becoming Canute's brother-in-law twice over. How-ever, as recent examinations of her skeleton have revealed, Estrid was ungainly, deformed and had protruding teeth. She was soon cast off and a third wife became mother to Richard's children. As al-ready mentioned, Estrid later married Ulf Jarl and became mother to Sweyn Estridsen.

So much for William the Conqueror's lineage, but before continuing with his career we shall devote a few lines to the population of Normandy at that time. The term Norman does not mean Norwegian, but merely 'men from the north' and, though Rollo was possibly Norwegian and not Danish, there is no doubt that the great majority of the Vikings who had settled in Normandy round about Rollo's time were Danish. Both historical and linguistic sources bear witness to this.

A number of place-names in Normandy obvi-ously conceal good Danish ones: out of the 82 Norman place-names containing Nordic personal names that were listed during the period prior to 1066, 26 are typically Danish and only 2 Norwegian; while the remainder could be either.

The population in Normandy was then – and to some degree still is – characterised by a marked Nordic strain. Yet despite his tall powerful stature William the Conqueror himself was not typically Nordic. In the Bayeux Tapestry he is portrayed a total of 17 times in widely different situations. The composite picture of him presents an almost southern European physiognomy with black hair, dark eyes, a straight 'Greek' nose and a rounded energetic chin. A contemporary written charac-terisation, of William's inner attributes also, is quoted on page 34.

William goes underground

In 1037 news came to Rouen of Duke Robert's death abroad and, as enjoined, the worthy Her-luin married William's young mother. There are indications that he had been living with her for some years by that time (see page 35). He became, or was already, through her the father of William's two stepbrothers, Odo (of Bayeux) and Robert (of Mortain).

The peace that had hitherto prevailed in Nor-mandy ended abruptly upon the news of Duke Robert's death. A number of the barons who had solemnly sworn allegiance to William left the court and hastened to their farms, which they turned into strongholds for their forthcoming struggles against each other and against the young Duke. Within the next three years the boy saw the good men to whom his father had entrusted his safety and welfare systematically eliminated by hateful rivals. The first to be murdered was William's guardian, Gilbert of Brionne. Thurold, his tutor, was the next to be stabbed to death by an unknown assailant. The killing of his grand seneschal took place uncomfortably close to him. Osbern was murdered in his bed in the castle Le Vaudreuil while the boy slept beside him, unnoticed by the assassins. In this case the ringleader, William of Montgomery, and his accomplices were pursued by Osbern's Nordic bailiff, Bjørn, and they were all killed. Finally in 1040 one of William's supreme protectors, his uncle Count Alain of Brittany, died after having been poisoned.

At this time William's adherents found it wiser to have the boy 'go underground'; and while he was growing up during the next five or six years nothing was heard of him. French history writers could only relate that he was probably placed anonymously in the care of some poor farm labourers or wood-cutters. They seem to have protected the young Duke conscientiously against a harsh world in a way his high-born guardians could not.

During these years, while William was building up his strength to challenge his opponents, there were perfidious intrigues and bloody feuds all over the duchy. When he finally felt ready to appear on the scene again, one of his first actions was to capture his birthplace, Falaise. There the castle was in the hands of a certain Toustain, son of Ansfred the Dane. William appealed with success to the citizens and knights in the city that had housed his father and fostered his mother. Before a day was over, the loyal forces had liberated the town and had driven Toustain to flight.

At this juncture, in 1046, a group of nobles with William's own cousin Guy of Brionne among its leaders conspired against the life of the young Duke. Guy was the son of William's paternal aunt Adelisa and Count Renaud of Burgundy, and he felt that he was just as much entitled to the ducal tide as his cousin. The conspirators had their headquarters in Bayeux where William's faithful jester Gollet happened to be staying at the time, while his master himself changed his abode every night. Gollet got wind of the conspiracy to murder the Duke. After nightfall he went to the little town of Valognes where he knew that William was spending the night, though he did not know which house he was in. He banged on all the doors in the village and shouted at the top of his

William the Conqueror is described in The Anglo-Saxon Chronicle by a monk who 'having ourselves seen him and at one time dwelt in his court' as a 'man of great wisdom and power, who surpassed in honour and in strength all those who had gone before him.' This section of the Bayeux Tapestry shows the Duke in the characteristic pose which is known from so many portraits of rulers during the early Middle Ages; dignified, erect, with feet together and knees apart, drawn up high. The sword – symbol of power and justice – rests in his right hand.

voice that the Duke should flee for his life. William heard him, mounted his horse and hurried out of the town. In the outskirts of Bayeux he entered a church to pray for strength. On coming out he noticed a party of horsemen galloping past in the dark towards Valognes. He did not dare to stop in Bayeux now and roamed about all night, until a faithful knight and his son led him safely to Falaise.

Threatened by powerful enemies within his own dukedom, William now clutched at a straw. Had not his father placed him under the protection of his feudal overlord, the very King of France?

True enough, Henry I had also fished in troubled waters during these last years of unrest and had gained influence over eastern Normandy. Yet now that the courageous and resolute young Duke had invoked his aid, he acknowledged his responsibility towards his 20-year-old vassal.

The Duke wins his rights

Soon after in the valley of Val-ès-Dunes between Caen and Falaise two armies of cavalrymen clashed. William's host of loyal adherents with their French allies led by the King himself faced the rebel forces only a couple of hundred yards away.

Battle broke out. It was short and violent. The conspirators were killed or forced to flee. William, who was already an accomplished rider and a practised swordsman, is said to have fought so well in his first pitched battle that King Henry knighted him on the spot. After the conflict was decided, William demonstrated one of his typical qualities. just as he could be relentless, indeed even brutal, in resisting attack, in victory he could be magnanimous towards the vanquished and humiliated. Apart from a few of the most villainous ringleaders in the conspiracy, all were pardoned. This move may have been dictated just as much by political astuteness as by humanity. His cousin, Guy of Brionne, was in time forgiven and retired to Burgundy.

By his victory at Val-ès-Dunes, William finally ensured his power in the dukedom over which he had formally been ruler for a decade. In 1051, the year when the strong man of England, Earl Godwin, was living in exile in Flanders (see page 22), the Duke crossed the Channel. Strangely enough, the Norman writers are silent regarding this event. *The Anglo-Saxon Chronicle* merely devotes a few lines thus: '(Then soon) came Duke William from beyond the sea with a great retinue of Frenchmen, and the King received him and as many of his companions as it pleased him, and let him go again.' It was apparently a totally secret diplomatic mission, yet if this visit really took place, it must have been the occasion when Edward the Confessor promised him the crown of England should he himself die without issue, according to what William subsequently maintained. Edward, whose Norman upbringing and sympathies have already been mentioned, could very well have been persuaded by his young relative to make such a promise at precisely this time, when the only two Anglo-Saxons who might have prevented it, Godwin and his son Harold, were in disfavour.

The determined suitor

With his self-confidence increasing, William went courting. He sought the hand of the daughter of Count Balduin of Flanders, Matilda, whose sister Judith was already married to Harold Godwinson's brother Tostig. An alliance between powerful Normandy and its wealthy neighbour to the east Flanders would strengthen William's position externally. However, the courtship did not go quite smoothly. It is said that when William's envoys conveyed their message to the court in Lille, the beautiful and wise (apparently all great men's wives were so at that time), though proud damsel replied arrogantly: 'I would rather take the veil than give myself to a bastard!'

However, she did not know this William who was later, not for nothing, to be called the Conqueror. When he heard her answer, he rode off in a fury directly to Lille and forced his way into the Count's castle. Before the eyes of her father, he caught Matilda by the hair, dragged her to the ground and treated her to the toe-caps of his boots and spurs. If the legend is true, his resolute behaviour apparently impressed the damsel, and it is a fact that she married him and remained true to him until his death 30 years later. William too was faithful to her; unlike many of his ancestors, he kept no mistresses, neither before nor after entering matrimony.

However, even before the marrige Pope Leo IX imposed a ban on the alliance, claiming that William and Matilda were too close of kin. They really were related, but so distantly that even the strictest ecclesiastical authority would normally have granted dispensation. (William was, as already mentioned, the great-great-greatgrandchild of Rollo, and Matilda that of Rollo's sister.) The papal opposition arose rather from political reasons. William flatly refused to accept separation, so both he and the whole of Normandy were excommunicated. It was a frightful sanction to impose upon a population both deeply religious and superstitious. They were thereby excluded from the almost vital services of the Church.

Six years passed before a new Pope, Nicholas II, eventually recognised William's marriage, but it is not known whether the excommunication was actually maintained so long. William's friend and advisor Lanfranc, 20 years his senior, who was the prior of the monastery in Le Bec and founder of the learned academy there, had been in Rome where he had triumphed in a controversy in the Lateran Council. The wise prior, who was born in Pavia, took up William's case and convinced the Pope that should Count Balduin be forced to take back his 'misused' daughter, the insult could lead to a bloody war between these two vassal states of France. Furthermore, William was firmly resolved to keep Matilda!

The price for papal absolution was high: The ducal couple would have to establish hospitals for the old, the sick and the blind in Rouen, Caen, Bayeux and Cherbourg. William would have to erect and maintain a monastery, and Matilda a convent. The result can still be seen in Caen in the two Romanesque establishments of the Abbaye-aux-Hommes and the Abbaye-aux-Dames.

William and Matilda had at least eight children in their marriage, four sons and four daughters. The eldest son Robert – called 'Courte-heuse' (short-hose) in the contemporary almost Dano-French language, because of his short legs – was followed by Richard, William Rufus (or the Red) and Henry Beauclerc. Two of them, William Rufus and Henry (the First), succeeded their father as Kings of England. The daughters were called Constance, Adelaide, Adelisa (or Agatha) and Adela. One became prioress of Matilda's convent

Lanfranc, William's mentor and friend of many years' standing, was born in Pavia, Italy. After having studied the sciences, he travelled as a teacher. In 1039 he settled in Normandy where an academy grew up around him. Acknowledging his own vanity, he suddenly broke off this activity to become a monk in the Norman monastery of Le-Bec-Hellouin. There after some years of study of the Holy Scriptures, he again gathered pupils about him from all of western Europe. It was probably at this time that young Duke William came into contact with him. In 1045 Lanfranc became prior in Bec. In 1066 he followed William to England where in 1070 he became Archbishop of Canterbury. He was responsible for persuading the Pope to rank the Archbishop of Canterbury higher than the Archbishop of York. This was achieved by means of falsified documents, although he himself was not the originator of them. Miniature c. 1100 in the Bodleian Library, Oxford.

in Caen and two were married to French noble-men, while Adelisa died unmarried after having been a pawn in the game for the throne of England; more about this later (page 49).

'His voice could be harsh...'

During the period before William's marriage was recognised, he was constantly involved in violent conflicts. In 1054 his good helper at Val-ès-Dunes, King Henry I of France, annulled the old feudal charter granted Rollo by Charles the Simple, and tried to gain control of Normandy. Orderic Vital describes the incident briefly as follows:

'At the instigation of Satan, who never ceases to harm people, a violent conflict flared up between the French and the Normans. King Henry of France and the brave Count Gotfred Martel of Anjou invaded Normandy with a powerful host and inflicted great losses on the Normans. However, the bold Duke William of Normandy was not slow to avenge the injury many times over. He captured most of the Gauls and the Angevins, killed some of them and let many languish in prison for a long time.'

'The bold Duke William', then King of England, was described a few years after his death by an anonymous monk from Caen, who gave an extremely vivid picture of a personality both pragmatic and dynamic:

'This king surpassed all the princes of his time in wisdom and he dominated them by the greatness of his spirit. He was never deterred from carrying out any enterprise because of the labour entailed and was always dauntless in the face of danger. He was extremely knowledgeable when assessing the importance of any event. He was able in both adversity and success to derive full benefit from fickle fortune. He was large of build, strong, tall, but not clumsy. He was moderate as regards food and drink, particularly the latter, as he detested drunkenness in anyone, despising it most in himself and at his court. He was so temperate in his consumption of wine and other drink that after his mealtime he seldom drank more than

three times. His speech was fluent and convincing, always able to express his will. If his voice could be harsh, what he said was always suitable for the occasion. He followed the tenets of Christianity in which lie had been brought up from his childhood...'

William had to fight against rebellious vassals and aggressive princely neighbours almost unceasingly, yet always successfully. After the death of King Henry I in 1060, and when William had conquered the province of Maine to the south of his own in 1062, the Duke of Normandy had become the most powerful man in all northern France.

This was the position he held when one day in 1064 he received an urgent message that his vassal Count Guy in Ponthieu, the region round the Somme estuary, had imprisoned the English Earl Harold Godwinson – William's most dangerous rival in the struggle for power in England – upon the stranding of his ship on the Count's coast.

However, this is already encroaching on the narrative in the Bayeux Tapestry which is soon to begin. There remains one further preliminary: a presentation of Duke William's stepbrother Odo, whose greatest significance in this connection is that by all accounts it was he who had this invaluable historical piece of evidence produced.

Bishop Odo
and the Bayeux Tapestry

After the news of Duke Robert's death, Count Herluin of Conteville married William's mother Arletta. She bore him two sons, Odo and Robert, as Norman historians relate.

One might wonder why the Duke had chosen one of his less significant vassals to be stepfather to his son, and why he had not himself married Arletta before his departure, thus removing any grounds for the nickname of 'the Bastard'. The explanation might perhaps be found in the early twelfth-century account by the English monk and historian William of Malmesbury, which suggests that Herluin and

Arletta were already married before Robert's death! If Odo was born after Duke Robert's death, e.g. between 1035 and 1038, he could only have been 12 to 15 years old when the new Duke, his stepbrother William, appointed him Bishop of Bayeux in about 1050. Experts in church history say that the appointment of so young a bishop would have been a scandal which would inevitably have occasioned violent protests from ecclesiastical quarters. An age of about 20 years might have been acceptable. If Odo were 20 in 1050, he must have been born in about 1030, i.e. several years before Duke Robert's departure. If this holds good, it indicates that already a few years after William was born, Robert had given up the liaison with Arletta, who thereupon attached herself to Herluin.

Odo developed into a strong personality and performed his ecclesiastical functions with great enthusiasm. In 1059 he founded a monastery in Troarn, and he soon set about completing the cathedral in Bayeux commenced by his predecessor. He was able to conclude the work in 1077.

As mentioned earlier, it was for this occasion – the consecration of the large and beautiful cathedral – that the Bayeux Tapestry seems to have been made. Bishop Odo occupies a prominent place in the tapestry's narrative – he appears as a central figure in four scenes. His efforts both before and after the Battle of Hastings were richly rewarded by William the Conqueror. Shortly after the victory he was given the town of Dover and awarded the title of Earl of Kent.

The Chronicle relates that when King William was away in his Duchy of Normandy, Odo was his regent in England. There was substance behind his authority. According to the *Domesday Book*, William's great register of English landed property from 1086, Odo was the largest landowner in England after the King, even greater than his brother, Robert of Mortain, who owned nearly 800 estates in 20 counties! Power was necessary to maintain Norman rule in the first turbulent decades after the conquest. As early as 1067, Odo had to crush an uprising in Kent. It was as the King's deputy that in 1077 he put down a bloody

Bishop Odo of Bayeux, son of William's mother Arletta and the knight Herluin of Conteville, was just as energetic in church affairs as in politics, but his ambitions brought about his downfall. His features are reproduced in the Bayeux Tapestry in strangely different versions. Here he is pictured as a thin, ascetic and serious person. In a subsequent portrait (see page 6) he is shown as a round-cheeked and almost jovial cherubic soul. Beside him is a ship's carpenter. The versatile Bishop took part in the entire battle at Hastings, armed with a stout club. As a priest he could not wield a sword; is it not written: "All they that take the sword shall perish with the sword" (Math. 26: 52)? There is no mention of iron-studded clubs.

revolt at a place called Fagadon. After the death of William Fitz-Osbern, who had been William the Conqueror's governor in Northumbria, Odo also undertook to keep order in the north of England, during the King's absence. He quelled a rebellion there in 1080 with great brutality and at the same time even ransacked a couple of churches and monasteries.

However, Odo was not merely a zealous viceroy, he was an even keener churchman. His vanity and ambition in this field were his undoing.

Pope Gregory VII had first triumphed over the Emperor Henry IV in a dispute over the right to appoint church officials (and Henry had to wear sackcloth and ashes and walk to Canossa!). In the next round the Pope was forced to flee from Rome and Henry chose a weak 'anti-pope', Clement III, whereupon Odo cast envious eyes towards the Holy See.

Orderic Vital relates that certain Roman soothsayers had predicted that a man by the name of Odo would become Pope after Gregory's death. 'When Bishop Odo of Bayeux heard this, he reckoned that the power and might of a kingdom in the west was worthless if it could not enable him to become pope and extend his dominion over all the people in the whole world. Therefore he sent envoys to Rome, bought a palace there and won over the senators of the Quirinal with lavish gifts…'

In 1082 while William was staying in Normandy, Odo mustered a large host of knights on the Isle of Wight, with Earl Hugo of Chester at their head, and urged them and their retainers to accompany him to Rome. 'And since the Normans are always fickle and desirous of seeing foreign countries, they immediately agreed with the overbearing bishop.'

The ambitious Bishop is arrested

As soon as William heard about Odo's doings, he rushed to the Isle of Wight, and before a council of thanes he accused his stepbrother of abusing his powers. He had learned of Odo's outrageous acts in Northumbria and upbraided him sharply for them. What was even worse was that Odo had tried to persuade knights, whose duty it was to protect England, to break their oath to the King and leave the country.

William thereafter ordered Odo's arrest and Orderic Vital relates that when none of those present dared to lay hands on the mighty man, the King himself came forward and took hold of him.

'I am a priest, I am a servant of God!' shouted Odo excitedly. 'A bishop cannot be tried except by the Pope!'

'It is neither as a priest nor as a bishop that I am condemning you,' answered William. 'It is as my earl whom I have placed over my realm on my behalf that I am holding you to account!'

Odo was led away under guard, to be sent to Rouen where he was imprisoned in the city fortress.

Although many in England interceded on Odo's behalf, including his brother Robert of Mortain, William was adamant. He characterised Odo as being superficial, spiteful, ambitious and addicted to pleasures of the flesh, and he foresaw that he might again cause disaster for England.

Not until William's death in 1087 was Odo set free. None of the Bishop's enormous estates in England had been confiscated, nor was he deprived of his title as Earl of Kent. He was fully accepted by the new King, William Rufus, but the Conqueror proved right in his dire prophesies.

Hardly had William Rufus been crowned than Odo instigated a conspiracy against him in favour of the King's brother, Robert Shorthose, who himself was striving for the throne. Bishops and earls attacked royal castles, burning and plundering where they could. The King succeeded in persuading a sufficient number of earls to rally round him with an army by promising them generous rewards. Thereafter he laid siege to the fortress of Pevensey where Odo had sought refuge. When at last the Bishop gave up his resistance, he agreed to accompany the King's men to his own castle in Rochester to arrange for its surrender. However, the castle garrison captured both Odo and the King's soldiers. The King now appealed to all honest men in the country, both English and French, to help in a final confrontation. After a siege the castle surrendered and Odo escaped across the sea, but this time he lost all his privileges in England. The next time – and the last – we hear about Odo is when he had left on a journey to the Holy Land together with his nephew Robert Shorthose who himself had participated without success in the plot against William Rufus. He died in Palermo in

For centuries the cathedral in Bayeux was the setting for the long pictorial hanging for which the pompous Bishop Odo is given the honour. In this place of worship the local citizens on festive occasions could dwell upon the historic memories presented in the following pages. Photo: M. R.

Sicily in 1097 without having returned either to his birthplace, Normandy, or to England, the country which he had helped to conquer.

Neither Odo nor any of his contemporaries have left any mention of the tapestry with which he is credited today. If he actually ordered its production and decided its themes, we cannot but commend the impartial rendering of the historical events. His admired and apparently envied stepbrother, William the Conqueror, is depicted both loyally and in good measure. Odo himself is prominent, but does not predominate. The English warriors appear just as heroic as the French.

Could it perhaps be because of Odo or that the artist behind the Bayeux Tapestry supposedly was English that Harold Godwinson is treated with unmistakable sympathy?

The Bayeux Tapestry narrative

In the following 52 pages the entire Bayeux Tapestry is reproduced in about one-sixth of its original size, in colours as close to the natural as is technically possible with this reduction in size. The 900 years and more during which the long wall hanging has been in existence have left their mark. However, despite spots of discoloration and repairs to holes and rents, even this modest-scale reproduction presents a good impression of the colours and delineation of this unique work of art.

As mentioned in the opening chapter, it is of course particularly effective when, as in Bayeux, the entire hanging can be seen as a long continuous strip. However, in this book the endeavour is to divide the pictorial narrative into the individual scenes of which it is nevertheless composed. With each segment the accompanying Latin text is given together with a translation.

Diplomatic mission or ill-fated hunt?

The King of England, Edward the Confessor, had summoned his brother-in-law Harold Godwinson, the Earl of Wessex, to his Palace in Westminster to order him to go to Normandy. There he was to reaffirm officially to Duke William the promise given by King Edward many years earlier that William would succeed to the throne of England after Edward's death.

This is clearly the conception of the events conveyed by the Bayeux Tapestry. It confirms the account given by the Norman cleric, Guillaume de Poitiers – unless instead it was de Poitiers who based his evidence on the tapestry! The English chronicler William of Malmesbury, who wrote somewhat later, has a slightly different version of the story. He claims that while on a fishing trip

EDWARD REX. UBI HAROLD DUX ANGLORUM ET SUI MILITES EQUITANT AD BOSHAM.
King Edward. Where Harold, Earl of the English, and his retinue ride to Bosham.

Harold was driven by a storm on to the French coast, taken prisoner and that after some time, of his own volition he vowed to support the Duke. William's claim to the English throne which is the main theme of the Bayeux Tapestry was based by the Duke himself both on his close kinship with the childless King Edward – Edward was a cousin of William's father (see genealogical table on page 100) – and on the definite promise given him by the King in 1051 (see page 23).

The King is seen seated on his throne, which is adorned with animal heads and feet. His type of beard alone makes him seem older than Harold and his companions, who in the English fashion of the time sport only moustaches. The date was about 1064, when King Edward was about 61 years old and already marked by the illness which was to prove fatal less than two years later.

With his falcon in hand and his hounds dashing on ahead, Harold and his retinue ride to Bosham, a small coastal town between Chichester and Portsmouth, where he had his estate.

Hunting with falcons had come to Europe from Asia during the era of the great migrations in the fifth and sixth centuries. It had now become a widespread and favourite sport among princes and the nobility.

Scenes 1 and 2 are separated, like so many others, by a stylised tree with interlacing branches in a pattern which in Viking times was prevalent in Scandinavia, Ireland and England.

The inscription, although terse, provides posterity with invaluable information as to the persons and events depicted.

On the way, Harold and his companions pray in Bosham Church for a successful mission. The representation of architecture in the Bayeux Tapestry must not be taken too literally, yet the small, single-aisled, shingle-roofed building without a tower, gives some idea of an Anglo-Saxon village church of that time. Bosham Church still exists, greatly altered in its exterior, but with an interior in part unchanged from what Harold would have seen.

Harold and his men take a last meal at his estate. An outside stairway leads to the upstairs room where they are dining. The roof seems to be tiled. Conversation is lively, Harold is drinking from a bowl, another man from a drinking horn, when someone discreetly indicates that the wind is favourable…

The borders of the Bayeux Tapestry display a number of different subjects; some are animals, birds and supernatural creatures, others are illustrations of fables or scenes from farming and hunting.

Sloping bars alternate with small plants which have been interpreted as symbols of life.

In the middle of the lower border (above) there is an illustration of Aesop's fable about the raven, the fox and the piece of cheese.

While the crew hold the ship off the beach with poles and oars, Harold and his companions wade through the shallow water, bare-legged and with tunics girded up. Falcons and hounds are carried on board. One man is fixing the mast, another in the bow is holding the anchor, which is of the type we know from the Gokstad ship in Oslo and the Ladby ship in Funen (see pages 61 and 65 on the construction of the ships).

Below the ships is an illustration of Aesop's fable about the ape asking the lion, on behalf of the animals, to become their king. Do these symbolise Harold and William?

ECCLESIA. HIC HAROLD MARE NAVIGAVIT ET VELIS VENTO PLENIS VENIT IN TERRAM WIDONIS COMITIS.

The church. Here Harold took to sea and came with full sail to the territory of Count Guy.

HAROLD: hIC: APPRE

At first sight it looks as if five different ships are represented as taking part in the expedition, but more probably it is the same ship that is depicted at various stages of the voyage. Harold himself is at the helm. One man is climbing up the mast to keep a look-out, two men are poling, while one is taking soundings.

Finally the anchor is cast. The landing place is near the estuary of the river Somme, on the estate of William's vassal, Count Guy of Ponthieu. The mast is lowered and the ship is nearly empty when something dramatic occurs. Guillaume de Poitiers describes it:

'Whilst travelling upon this errand Harold only escaped the perils of the sea by making a forced landing on the coast of Ponthieu where he fell into the hands of Count Guy…'

The Bayeux Tapestry does not indicate any forced landing in heavy weather, yet there is no doubt that Harold landed on his enemy's shore where, according to old custom, he was liable to be plundered, imprisoned and held for ransom. Now the Count arrives with an armed following even before all the voyagers have donned their hose again. There is no doubt about the seriousness in the Count's threatening gesture, and Earl Harold has hastily drawn his sax – a combined dagger and eating knife which could be used in an emergency as a defensive weapon.

Harold is now led under escort to Count Guy's castle in Beaurain, he rides ahead with falcon in hand, followed by Guy, likewise with a falcon. In the rear are two Englishmen and three Normans – the former recognisable by their moustaches, the latter by their characteristic hair fringe and clean-shaven nape.

The horses' harnesses include stirrups, a simple but important contrivance first introduced into Europe after Roman times from Asia, the homeland of horsemanship. The riders have their legs almost straight in the stirrups to help them keep their balance when using sword or lance or when putting their body weight behind the throwing of a spear. Spurs are of the goad type – the wheel spur came much later on in the Middle Ages.

HAROLD. HIC APPREHENDIT WIDO HAROLDUM ET DUXIT EUM AD BELREM ET IBI EUM TENUIT.
Harold. Here Guy seized Harold and led him to Beaurain and kept him there.

We have not previously seen Harold with a sword, but the one which the tall Norman is holding in his hand might well be the Earl's, which he had had to unbuckle when surrendering. In the next scene, in which Harold and another Englishman are in animated conversation with Count Guy, who is now enthroned on his high seat, the Earl has got back his sword.

At Guy's left arm a man is clearly trying to draw the Count's attention to something – could it be the person eavesdropping behind the pillar at the right of the hall? Sometimes he is described as a 'spy', and perhaps it is he who secretly informed Duke William about Guy's coup.

The designer of the tapestry has transposed the next three scenes. The chronological order of the events is that a messenger tells William about Harold's capture (page 46, above), the Duke sends a couple of horsemen to Beaurain (page 45, below), where on behalf of the Duke they demand the handing over of the English Earl (page 45, top right).

This time Count Guy is supported by his long-handled battle-axe, a weapon and symbol of authority which, as seen later, is to a much greater degree characteristic of the Anglo-Saxons rather than the Normans.

While a bearded dwarf holds the snorting steeds William's envoys convey their demand to the Count and presumably one of his advisors. The taller messenger is one of the few minor characters in the Bayeux Tapestry who is named. He is called Turold (Thorald) and must have been generally known at the time.

Below to the right, Duke William's envoys gallop off with their hair flying in the wind.

On both their shields are winged dragons with forelegs and knotted serpents' tails. The dragon, a favourite figure on weaponry in Europe since the days of Imperial Rome, appears in the Bayeux Tapestry with both Normans and Anglo-Saxons.

The frieze below shows ploughing with a wheel plough, sowing and harrowing. Further to the right: a man hunts birds with a sling, and finally the popular pastime of bear-baiting. Above in the same section are two female centaurs.

UBI HAROLD (ET) WIDO PARABOLANT. UBI NUNTII WILLELMI DUCIS VENERUNT AD WIDONEM. TUROLD. NUNTII WILLELMI.

Where Harold and Guy converse. Where Duke William's messengers came to Guy. Turold [Thorald]. William's messengers.

HIC VENIT NUNTIUS AD WILGELMUM DUCEM.
HIC WIDO ADDUXIT HAROLDUM AD WILGELMUM NORMANNORUM DUCEM.
Here the messenger came to Duke William.
Here Guy took Harold to William, Duke of Normandy.

Here we are at the beginning of the sequence in the wrong order. A look-out up a tree may be announcing the messenger from Beaurain, half-kneeling while giving his report to Duke William, who is shown here for the first time. The messenger seems to be English and might conceivably be one of Harold's men who had avoided capture.

Unlike Guy, William sits on a cushion on his high seat. Below his knees he is wearing very unusual garters with broad tassels.

The incident probably takes place in the open (notice the 'sign' of grass or cobblestone under the messenger) in front of the castle in Rouen, which is shown to the right in an elaborate and fanciful rendering with guards posted behind the crenellated battlements.

In the hunting scene in the border below, a huntsman is holding back a couple of his hounds and sounding his horn.

We do not know whether Count Guy gave up his distinguished prisoner under pressure from his liege lord, or whether the Duke had to ransom Earl Harold. However, in the next scene Guy leads Harold to Rouen and the Duke rides out to meet them. Both parties are accompanied by armed men.

Guy is riding a strange-looking mount, perhaps a mule. He is pointing back at Harold who is now equipped with spurs. Guy and Harold are wearing short cloaks, William's cloak is longer and with two tassels at the neck.

Above there are two camels; below to the left a naked man and woman face each other; their significance is not known. To their right are two dragons.

HIC·DVX·VVILGELM·CVM hAROLDO·VENIT·ADPA LATIV SVV

Guest or prisoner?

A guard on the city gate or castle tower in Rouen sees Harold and William approaching.

The next episode takes place in a hall under a long arcade. William is enthroned on a high seat. Behind him stands a Norman, armed with a spear, who apparently takes part in the Duke's conversation with the English Earl, who on his side is seconded by one of his men. On the far right stand three of the Duke's bodyguards with spears and (four!) shields.

It is evident that in this vivid scene a lively discussion is going on, and that it is Harold who is talking at the moment. Is he carrying out his King's orders – to confirm Edward's promise of the English throne to the Duke – or is the artist indicating that the Earl is protesting against the imprisonment to which English writers have later claimed he was subjected? Contemporary French historians, however, stress William's friendly attitude and de Poitiers says, for instance: 'William sumptuously refreshed Harold with splendid hospitality after all the hardships of his journey. For the Duke rejoiced to have so illustrious a guest in a man who had been sent him by the nearest and dearest of his friends…'

In the top border there are, among other things, two peacocks; below, a naked man is sharpening a broad-edged axe.

To the far right of the main picture is an inexplicable scene which has given rise to many conjectures, but no satisfactory interpretation. In a doorway surmounted by two carved animal heads, stands a wellborn young lady wearing a long dress reaching down to her feet. She is making a defensive gesture with her left hand while 'a clerk' – his tonsure indicates that he is a priest – extends his right hand towards her face. It is difficult to decide whether this is a sign of affection or whether he is chastising her.

It is as if the lack of a verb in the inscription 'where a certain clerk and Ælfgyva' is an implication of 'you know!', indicating that the significance of the episode was known and understood by everyone at the time it was depicted in the tapestry. Perhaps it hints at some scandal or other. The naked, almost obscene man below, in nearly the same posture as the clerk, might imply something of that sort. In any case, what has it to do with all the rest of the story? Ælfgyva is merely another spelling of Ælfgifu which we have encountered several times already, and is a purely

HIC DUX WILGELM CUM HAROLDO VENIT AD PALATIUM SUUM. UBI UNUS CLERICUS ET ÆLFGYVA.
HIC WILLELM DUX ET EXERCITUS EJUS VE(NERUNT AD MONTEM MICHAELIS).
Here Duke William comes to his palace with Harold. Where a certain clerk and Ælfgyva.
Here Duke William and his army came to Mont Saint Michel.

Anglo-Saxon name. Harold's youngest sister was called Ælfgifu, and according to tradition was promised to one of the Duke's vassals during her father's negotiations with William. But she could hardly have been present in Rouen at that point of time – nor did she go there subsequently. French quarters assume that the damsel is William's daughter Adelisa, who became engaged to Harold during his stay in Normandy (see page 55) and in such a case would have been given an English name. In the Bayeux Tapestry we see an adult woman, and as we know that the marriage was deferred just because the girl was not of age, this could not have been her either. The mystery will no doubt remain unsolved.

During Harold's stay in Normandy, William embarked on a campaign against Count Conan of Brittany, his neighbour to the south-west, and allowed his guest to take part in the expedition (the scene begins on page 49).

In the background is the monastery of Mont Saint Michel, lying off the estuary of the river Couesnon, which here forms the boundary between Normandy and Brittany. A horseman pulls up his feet to avoid getting them wet while fording the estuary. The area is still notorious for its quicksands and here there is trouble. A rider is thrown and Harold Godwinson rescues two panic-stricken Normans from perishing in the quicksands. The Bayeux Tapestry gives him full credit for this deed.

In 1064 Count Conan was fighting some Breton rebels and one of them, Riwallon of Dol, asked William for help. This was a welcome chance for the Duke to demonstrate his might against Conan, who is said to have been opposed to his English plans.

The Normans attack Dol and Conan escapes from the stronghold by means of a rope. Here is one of the few notorious errors in the tapestry's account of historical events: when William came to the aid of Riwallon, Conan had not yet captured the castle but had only laid siege to it. Therefore he did not flee from the castle itself as is represented so graphically, but was merely forced to lift the siege and retire.

As with all the other architectural works in the Bayeux Tapestry, the representation of the Dol stronghold is more a product of fantasy than a faithful reproduction. The impression is given that it lies on a height, or behind ramparts, and that the drawbridge is raised. Before his flight, Conan had barricaded the castle entrance with shields. The two birds possibly symbolise a peaceful surrender. Sheep are grazing on the slope in front of the castle in Rennes where the building itself consists of a central tower behind a palisade.

At the end of the upper border on page 49 are two specimens of the Amphisbaena – a mythical dragon with a head on either end. In the lower border (above) there are two griffins – having the

head and the wings of an eagle but the body of a lion. Eels and other fish represent the fauna of the estuary. They are also interpreted as being symbols of the constellations, Pisces and Serpents, and the following figures as Bootes, Arctus Major, Aquila, Lupus and Centaurus.

ET HIC TRANSIERUNT FLUMEN COSNONIS. HIC HAROLD DUX TRAHEBAT EOS DE ARENA.
ET VENERUNT AD DOL ET CONAN FUGA VERTIT. REDNES.
And here they crossed the river Cuesnon. Here Earl Harold pulled them out of the sands.
And they came to Dol, and Conan fled. Rennes.

(HIC MILIT)ES WILLELMI DUCIS PUGNANT CONTRA DINANTES ET CUNAN CLAVES PORREXIT.
Here Duke William's soldiers fight against the inhabitants in Dinan, and Conan handed over the keys.

Count Conan has fled on to Dinan, north-west of Rennes, and William's cavalry now attack this town. Here too the drawbridge is raised and a vivid impression is given of the fierce resistance put up by the defenders.

In the same picture three phases of the combat are depicted. The city gate is attacked, two soldiers set fire to the woodwork of the fortification, and finally Conan capitulates, handing over the city keys on the end of his lance to the Duke who receives them on the end of his. Thus neither of the two opponents has been within reach of the other's weapon.

William is shown here with his calves clad in chain mail. Later on he is the only man so protected, apart from his banner-bearer at Hastings.

To the left of the lower scene is one of the culminating points of Harold Godwinson's stay with William. In recognition of the Earl's participation in the Brittany campaign, the Duke presents him with a complete military outfit, a coat of mail, a helmet, a sword and a lance with 'gonfanon', and a banner, thereby signifying that Harold is now 'his man', under obligation to serve him. Harold's sword is thrust through a slit in the chain mail, just as is customary with the sabre in the uniform cloak of later times.

At last William and Harold return from the successfully concluded campaign in Brittany. Both are still fully accoutred for war as they ride into Bayeux, where the fortress is just as stylistically depicted as all other buildings in the tapestry.

The two eagles represent the emblem of the chapter of the city's cathedral at that time.

HIC WILLELM DEDIT ARMA HAROLDO. HIC WILLELM VENIT BAGIAS

Here William gave Harold weapons. Here William came to Bayeux

UBI HAROLD:SACRAMENTUM:FECIT:~ HIC HAROLD:DU
VUILLELMO DVCI:~

The costly oath

The next scene illustrates a crucial point in the whole drama concerning the conflict about the future rule of England.

'When they had come together in conference at Bonneville, Harold in that place swore fealty to the Duke employing the sacred ritual recognised among Christian men…' Guillaume de Poitiers' version is in disagreement about the locality where the famed oathtaking occurred, the tapestry places it in Bayeux.

William is enthroned and is making an admonitory gesture with his left hand towards Harold who is standing giving his oath, flanked by two reliquaries.

Behind the Duke stand two Normans who are obviously absorbed in the episode. To the right are two of Harold's companions, the more distant one providing the transition to the next scene of the voyage home, while the other who is also observing the sacred act with great attention seems to be making a warning sign with his right hand. There is nothing in the tapestry narrative, nor in contemporary French accounts, to indicate that Harold might have sworn insincerely. Nevertheless, later tradition recounts that after the cere-mony William revealed that the two caskets contained some particularly powerful relics. These were the bones of two English missionaries who had once fled to France and were martyred there, and that Harold was both horrified and embittered at having been 'tricked'.

The two reliquaries are both shaped like buildings, presumably churches – compare the one on the left with Bosham Church on page 40. Its two shafts make it portable and it could be the one that William took with him on his travels, and which after 1066 he had presented to Battle Abbey in England.

In *Harold Hardrada's Saga* the apparently well-informed Snorre presents a vivid account of an episode during Harold Godwinson's stay with William:

"Harold used to sit on the high seat on one side of the Duke, and on the Duke's other side sat the Duchess; she was the loveliest woman people had ever seen. The three of them always had a good time, drinking together; Duke William was usually the first to go to bed, but Harold used to stay up late into the night, talking with the Duchess. This went on for most of the winter.

Then on one occasion when the two of them

UBI HAROLD SACRAMENTUM FECIT WILLELMO DUCI. HIC HAROLD DUX REVERSUS EST AD ANGLI (CAM TERRAM).
Where Harold gave his oath to William. Here Earl Harold returned home to England.

were talking together, she said to Harold, 'The Duke has been speaking to me, and asking me what we are always talking about; he is beginning to get angry.'

Harold said, 'Then we must let him know at once what all our conversations have been about.'

Next day Harold went to see the Duke, and they went into the audience-chamber, where the Duchess and all his counsellors were waiting.

Harold said, 'I must inform you, sir, that there was more to my coming here than I have already told you: I wish to ask for the hand of your daughter in marriage. I have talked about this a great deal with her mother, and she has promised to support me in this proposal.'

As soon as Harold had made this known, it was well received by all those present and they pleaded the case with the Duke. Finally the girl was betrothed to Harold, but since she was still very young, it was agreed that the wedding should be postponed for a few years".

After his long visit to William, Harold returned home to England 'laden with gifts and accompanied right down to the shore by the Duke himself'. The house near the water, which his ship is approaching, could be his property in Bosham. Eager lookout for his vessel is kept from balcony, door and windows.

It is strange that neither Harold, who is presumably the tall figure beside the mast, nor any of his company have moustaches. Could this be due to the influence of French fashions or an omission on the part of the artist? Later on the English are apparently depicted at random with or without moustaches.

In the top border, above Harold's ship, is a pair of Pards or Manticoras, fabulous man-eating creatures with human faces, bodies of lions and poisonous stings like those of scorpions on the ends of their tails. Further to the right is Aesop's fable of the crane saving the wolf from choking.

Harold and a companion ride to London, which

is represented by a tower. A guard, armed with the long-handled 'Danish battle-axe', which we see here for the first time in the hands of an Englishman, announces Harold to the King. With every sign of humility, the Earl approaches King Edward, who looks ill and frail. With a crown on his head and staff in hand, the King asks his returning Earl and brother-in-law for a report.

Edward the Confessor is dead. His enshrouded body lies in a richly decorated bier borne by eight men to his final resting place in the Church of St. Peter, the Apostle. The procession consists of tonsured prelates, some with Prayer Books, others singing. Two acolytes carry bells.

A man is setting up the weathercock. This indicates that the church – later to be Westminster Abbey – has just been completed. The hand of God symbolises its consecration, which took place on 28 December 1065. The old King had been too frail to take part in the ceremony; he died a week later, on 5 January 1066, and was buried on the following day.

To the right is seen the event which immediately preceded this. It is not clear why the artist has reversed the order. Above, the dying King is sitting up in bed; the bed hangings are draped round the bed posts. He is supported by an attendant, while a courtier and a priest or bishop pay him sympathetic attention. At the end of the bed is the sorrowing Queen Edith, daughter of Earl Godwin and sister to Harold. It is tempting to believe that the man in the foreground is Harold himself, who presumably was present at the King's deathbed.

Below, two attendants prepare the dead King for burial under the supervision of a high prelate. The crown has now been removed – to reappear in the next scene.

ET VENIT AD EDWARDUM REGEM. HIC PORTATUR CORPUS EADWARDI REGIS AD ECCLESIAM SCI PETRI APOSTOLI.

HIC EADWARDUS REX IN LECTO ALLOQUITUR FIDELES. ET HIC DEFUNCTUS EST.

And came to King Edward. Here King Edward's body is carried to the Church of St. Peter the Apostle.

Here King Edward in bed speaks to his faithful. And here he died [Eadwardus is the Anglo-Saxon spelling].

The long-haired star

Two men are offering the crown of England to Harold Godwinson, and he is accepting it. All over Europe this succession stirred up interest, and it did not meet with general approval. The German historian Adam of Bremen – a close acquaintance of the Danish King Sweyn Estridsen – records the following in the *History of Hamburg Archbishops:* 'After the very pious English King Edward was dead, the thanes quarrelled over mastery of the realm and during this struggle an Anglo-Saxon Earl, Harold, an ungodly person, usurped the throne…'. These are harsh words about Harold, and are doubtless due largely to Adam's bitterness over England's increasing independence of the influence of the Hamburg archbishopric. There is nothing in the attitude or expression of the tall, masculine, 44-year-old Earl that indicates any overweening ambition. On the contrary, he seems to be carefully weighing up whether he should accept the offer. Here too we have an instance of the amazingly unbiased picture presented in the tapestry.

It is recounted that shortly before Edward died, he commended the welfare of his wife, his retainers and all his kingdom to the care of Harold.

This last point cannot be confirmed, but it is not unlikely that the frail childless King in his last moments might have forgotten his promise to Duke William, and appointed his favourite, kneeling at his bedside, as his heir.

Immediately after Edward's death, a Witenage-mot was convened in London, the purpose was to choose a new king.

There can hardly be any doubt that they all knew about the oath that Harold had given in Normandy. However, the view of the Witan was that since the Earl was not of royal Saxon blood, he was therefore not entitled to commit the realm either legally or morally; neither he nor the Witan could be bound by his promise to Duke William. Had Harold himself not said that the last wish of the old King was that Harold himself should be his successor? The word of a King was law and Harold Godwinson was thus chosen to be King Harold II.

In the next scene, King Harold is shown sitting majestically upon his throne with the crown on his head, the sceptre in his right hand and the orb in his left, receiving the homage of the people. At his left stands Archbishop Stigand of Canterbury. Actually, by all accounts it was the Archbishop Aldred of York who crowned the new King, but

HIC DEDERUNT HAROLDO CORONAM REGIS. HIC RESIDET HAROLD REX ANGLORUM.
STIGANT ARCHIEPISCOPUS. ISTI MIRANT STELLAM. HAROLD.
Here they gave the royal crown to Harold. Here enthroned is Harold, King of England.
Archbishop Stigand. These people marvel at the star. Harold.

that it was Stigand was a rumour which suited
the opponents in France very well. Stigand was at
that time excommunicated (he had received his
pallium, his symbol of office, from a schismatic
pope) and a religious ceremony performed by
him could therefore be declared invalid!

A group of people are watching from a building,
a flaming celestial body streaking over the roofs of
London. In the royal palace, an obviously agitated
person is reporting the evil omen to King Harold, who almost faints in horror. Below a fleet
of empty colourless vessels drift in the waves –
perhaps representing a vision or a dream had by
the King of William's invasion fleet which was at
that moment being built, or of his own ships with
which the yeomanry were to defend the south
coast of England but which had been taken out
of service shortly before the Normans landed (see
page 67).

'The Star' was the brilliant comet later known
as Halley's after the English eighteenth-century
astronomer Edmund Halley, who calculated its
orbit and predicted its return. Records of its
appearance go back to the year 466 BC when the
Chinese described it. It reappeared in 1910 and in
1985/86. Its coming in the spring of 1066 aroused
attention and consternation all over Europe. *The
Anglo-Saxon Chronicle* states:

'At that time, throughout all England, a portent
such as men had never seen before was seen in
the heavens. Some declared that the star was a
comet, which some call "the long-haired star": it
first appeared on the eve of the festival of Letania
major, that is on 24 April, and shone every night
for a week.'

HIC NAVIS ANGLICA VENIT IN TERRAM WILLELMI DUCIS.
HIC WILLELM DUX IUSSIT NAVES EDIFICARE.
Here an English ship came to Duke William's country.
Here Duke William ordered the building of ships.

'Build three thousand ships...'

Nor will lack of ships hinder us, for very soon we shall rejoice in the sight of a fleet... Wars are won not by numbers but by courage.

William, according to Guillaume de Poitiers

An English ship brings the news to Normandy of the latest events in England. A man informs William of Harold's coronation and thereby his violation of faith, and the Duke, in council with his stepbrother Bishop Odo, determines to build a fleet for the invasion of England. A ship's carpenter is already standing beside Odo with a broad-axe in hand.

This is the first appearance in the Bayeux Tapestry of Bishop Odo, its presumed originator. He is easily recognisable as a priest from his tonsure. His expression and gestures indicate that he, rather than his half-brother, whose inquiring glance is directed towards the dynamic Bishop, is taking the initiative.

In the middle of the picture three men are felling trees – shown rather more naturalistically than the stylised ones separating the individual scenes in the hanging. The next person is a carpenter sitting astride a beam to shape it with his broad-bladed axe. Behind him and above his head are piles of prepared planks.

The last five shipwrights in the picture are working on two vessels. The two above are young, one has a broad-axe and the other a drill. The person standing off the bow is a 'bow-wright', who is sighting to see whether the planks are in proper alignment. In wooden ship building, aesthetic and functional considerations complement each other. In Scandinavia, a bow-wright was paid twice as high a wage as a plank cutter. He was a specialist who decided the proportions and the lines of the ship.

Presumably for lack of space, the vessels here are also reproduced in unnaturally short form, but the use of various colours emphasises quite graphically the individual planks in the clinker-built boats.

HIC TRAHUNT NAVES AD MARE.

ISTI PORTANT ARMAS AD NAVES. ET HIC TRAHUNT CARRUM CUM VINO ET ARMIS.

Here they drag the ships to the sea.

These men carry weapons down to the ships. And here they pull a cart loaded with wine and weapons.

The ships are being launched. The men have taken off their hose; that the water barely reaches their knees indicates that even large vessels of this type rode high when unloaded – and even when loaded their draught was slight. The boats are moored here to the top of a high post – there is a great difference in water-level between high and low tide in these parts.

In the next scene, supplies of many kinds are being carried on board. Heavy coats of mail slung on poles are carried by two men on their shoulders.

Several of the men also carry weapons and helmets which they are holding by the nose-piece. One has an axe in his hand and a full wineskin over his shoulder. Another is carrying a barrel of wine. Two men in front are pulling a cart, with the wheel construction clearly shown. Each wheel-rim is made up of eight curved pieces of wood, one for each spoke. The cart is transporting a large barrel of wine – this expeditionary force really is made up of Frenchmen!

The English writer on the Bayeux Tapestry, Charles H. Gibbs-Smith, has pointed out that a coat of mail was not actually very heavy. It weighed from 12 to 14 kilos, and a fully equipped Norman warrior in battle order carried a total of 20 to 22 kilos. A modern soldier may have to carry about 25 kilos in the field.

At the far right William leads his men to the shore for embarkation.

In *Harald Hardrada's Saga*, Snorre presents a strange tale in connection with his description of William's departure:

'On the day that he was riding from the town down to the ships, he had just mounted his horse when his wife came over to him and tried to talk to him. When he saw her, he kicked at her with his heel; his spur plunged deep into her breast, and she fell down dead at once.'

Where Snorre got this cock-and-bull story about William's brutal behaviour towards his beloved wife is not known. Perhaps he had heard about his somewhat tempestuous courtship of Matilda (page 32), and possibly it is this legend that he has elaborated upon. At any rate Matilda in fact lived on in the best of health after William's departure and joined him in England in 1068.

The fleet lay ready in the Dives estuary and nearby harbours by 12 August 1066. However, the strong southerly breeze necessary for a speedy and direct crossing to the coast of southern England was not forthcoming. After a whole month had elapsed, a fierce storm broke from the west and the fleet was forced to move further east to take shelter in an excellent natural harbour, the estuary of the Somme. William had to wait another couple of weeks in the little local town of St. Valéry. Provisions were running low and the men getting disgruntled, when finally – in answer to the Duke's fervent prayers – the wind veered to the south. The fleet was ordered to put out immediately. It was 27 September.

Different sources give various figures for the numbers of ships, men and horses crossing the Channel between 27 and 28 September 1066. Guillaume de Jumiège writes that the fleet totalled 3,000 ships under William's command and his namesake from Poitiers states the size of the French army to be 50,000 men. Modern military historians, however, have established that these figures are impossible and that scarcely more than 450 ships took part in the expedition. A fleet of this size is still a considerable one, not least if one takes into account that most of the vessels were built between February and August of that same year.

The total number of men ferried across is now reckoned at 7,000 to 8,000 – noblemen, knights, ordinary soldiers, craftsmen, supply personnel, priests, grooms for the approximately 2,000 warhorses, and others.

The British military historian, Lieutenant-Colonel Charles H. Lemmon, who has gone deeply into the subject of the Norman invasion and the Battle of Hastings, has made a careful analysis of the timing of the embarkation, the crossing and the landing at Pevensey. He states that on the day of departure the sun set at 17.34 hrs. and that a six-day-old half-moon disappeared at 21.15 hrs. Because of the tide, it had been necessary to be on the open sea at 18.30 hrs. Next morning sunrise was at 6.04 hrs. Wind and weather conditions

(HIC WILLELM DUX IN MAGNO) NAVIGIO MARE TRANSIVIT ET VENIT...
(Here Duke William crosses in a big) ship over the sea and came...

seem to have been ideal and the fleet reached the English coast at Pevensey at about 8.30 hrs.

Along the gunwales of the finished ships there are rows of oar-ports where the oars could be shipped if the wind failed, just as the Danish and Norwegian Vikings had done for a couple of hundred years. That these were purely 'Viking ships' is also confirmed by their high bows and sterns decorated or fitted with carved animal heads. This type of 'dragon head' had also in earlier times been designed to be attached or removed as desired. The old Icelandic *Ulvjot Law* prescribes that people approaching new unbuilt-upon land 'at sea should not have ships with heads on them, but if they had, the heads should be detached before making landfall and not sail shoreward with jaws agape and grinning snouts so as to frighten the land spirits.' The land spirits were supernatural beings who were regarded as the original inhabitants and guardians of the land, with whom it was necessary to remain on good terms during and after settling on uninhabited land. Later the practice was to attach the heads when on a warlike mission, but to sail without heads, or to detach them, when approaching a friendly coast. In depicting Harold Godwinson's mission to Normandy (page 42), his ship's prow still carries a head after landing, and it must be assumed that the old rules were no longer valid in this respect.

The strangely placed shields in the bows of some of the ships are somewhat unsatisfactorily interpreted as protection against ramming by hostile craft.

The invasion

It would certainly have been ungrateful of William if he had really treated his wife as related by Snorre. The beautiful ship on which he himself sailed to England, larger and faster than all the others, had been a present to him from Matilda. Its name was 'Mora' and it can be seen to the left in the picture with William at the helm. There is a row of shields along the gunwale, an animal on the prow, and the figure of a boy in the stern pointing ahead with a banner while blowing a horn. The window-shaped object at the masthead could be the large lantern mentioned by Guillaume de Poitiers as the rallying point for the fleet during the nocturnal expedition.

In his vivid description of the crossing, Guillaume de Poitiers says that the Duke's ship quickly outsailed the others 'as if held to its course by the will of its master'. When daybreak came, none of the other ships in the fleet was in sight and 'in order to appease among his companions any fear or apprehension he commanded a large repast for himself, and accompanying it with a bumper of spiced wine he dined in good spirit as if he was in a room in his own house'.

At long last the other ships gathered round his and the voyage could continue.

Only two ships were lost on the way. At least one landed too far to the east, near the town of Romney, where the inhabitants killed all on board. In another the expedition's official soothsayer perished. The Duke did not regard this as any great loss considering that the man had not even been able to foresee his own unhappy end.

Actually the crossing of the mighty fleet was an extremely risky undertaking. The English Channel, which at that spot is about 100 km wide, can be a very stormy water-way, as many know from their own bitter experience. The wind could have freshened dangerously without warning – or dropped completely so that the crews would have had a long tiring row before them. The heavily-

HIC EXEVNT:CABALLI   DENAVIBVS·· ET HIC:MI

AD PEVENESÆ. HIC EXEUNT CABALLI DE NAVIBUS ET HIC...

...to Pevensey. Here the horses go ashore, and here...

laden vessels were poorly supplied with water and fodder for the horses, and at any rate were difficult to handle, with the risk of collision and disaster if they came too close to each other.

However, the greatest danger would have been a confrontation with King Harold's navy, which had been cruising in the waters off the Isle of Wight for some time, aware of the threat from the south. But because of the western storm already mentioned, Harold's fighting ships had been withdrawn from the south coast, and were now moored in the Thames undergoing repair of the damage they had suffered.

Most of the coastguards who had also been keeping a lookout to sea for a long time, were mainly of members of the 'fyrd' – militiamen who were farmers in daily life and therefore not to be called up for more than two months of the year. In his work, *A History of the English-Speaking Peoples*, Winston Churchill comments laconically about this: 'The local "fyrd" had been called out this year four times already to watch the coast, and having, in true English style, come to the conclusion that the danger was past because it had not yet arrived had gone back to their homes.'

Here on the right the tapestry shows a ship brought into such shallow water that the horses can spring ashore. In order to indicate that the horses are not merely standing before the boats, the artist has drawn the left hind leg of the animal in the rear still on board. The mast is being lowered. A number of unrigged craft without prow heads lie on the beach.

The landing in Pevensey Bay which started at 8.30 in the morning of 28 September proceeded without hindrance. The fyrd had been sent home at the beginning of September when crops would normally be harvested. Though the invaders met no resistance, they had at least been observed by the local thane as already mentioned, who reported three days later in York to King Harold (see page 28).

It is said that the only accident that happened was that Duke William stumbled and fell headlong as he jumped ashore. He got up at once, muddied, and exclaimed: 'Look, I have taken possession of England with both hands!'

Norman horsemen were sent out foraging for provisions.

The 'foraging soldiers', as the inscription for this scene reads, includes two bearing 'gonfanon' and all are clad in chain mail. They seem better suited to the reconnoitring done by William immediately after landing. In his mention of this episode, Guillaume de Poitiers gives an undoubtedly characteristic picture of the Duke as a military leader:

"Marius and Pompey the Great, both of whom earned their victories by courage and ability (since the one brought Jugurtha in chains to Rome whilst the other forced Mithridates to take poison), were so cautious when they were in enemy territory that they feared to expose themselves to danger even by separating themselves with a legion from their main army; like that of most generals their custom was to direct patrols and not to lead them. But William, with twenty-five knights and no more, himself went out to gain information about the neighbourhood and its inhabitants.

MILITES FESTINAVERUNT HESTINGAM UT CIBUM RAPERENTUR. HIC EST WADARD.
...the soldiers hurried to Hastings to requisition food. Here is Wadard.

Because of the roughness of the ground he had to return on foot, a matter doubtless for laughter, but if the episode is not devoid of humour it none the less deserves serious praise. For the Duke came back carrying on his shoulder, besides his own hauberk, that of William Fitz-Osbern, one of his companions. This man was famed for his bodily strength and courage, but it was the Duke who relieved him in his necessity of the weight of his armour".

Could it be that the foremost rider is the Duke himself, with his spear balanced lightly in his right hand, and behind him Fitz-Osbern who already looks tired?

The next scene shows some of the results of the foraging: an ox, presumably lying on the ground and perhaps having been struck on the head by the man with the axe; behind him another man with a sheep. To the right of the ox is a man carrying a circular object against his neck, possibly a loaf or a bundle of sorts, and another carrying a pig over his shoulder.

The mail-clad rider further to the right is one of the few persons in the Bayeux Tapestry mentioned by name. There is something ostentatious about this Wadard. He must have been of importance in this situation – perhaps responsible for the whole commissariat service? We do not know; but he could be the Wadard who later figures in William the Conqueror's land register, *the Domesday Book*, as a tenant of Bishop Odo.

In front of Wadard is a man leading a little packhorse.

The small buildings in the background could be modest English country houses.

The following scene is extraordinarily rich in details giving valuable information on the preparation and eating of a meal. The place is presumably Hastings and the time the day after the landing.

To the left two cooks are supporting a couple of forked branches suspending a large cauldron over flames licking up from a long-legged stove. There are a number of spits above with pieces of meat ready for roasting. To the right of the cooks, a baker is taking hot loaves or cakes from an oven with the aid of tongs and placing them on a tray.

These operations are going on in the open. The stylised portal, in front of which there are two helpers handling spits with roasted meat, indicates that the following proceedings take place indoors. A servant is receiving two birds cooked on spits at an improvised serving table made from two shields placed on trestles, while another is blowing a horn to announce the meal.

The next scene is the meal itself with the Norman 'staff' seated behind a curved table. The artist has succeeded in illustrating four stages of the same meal in a single picture (see full scale detail on page 6):

1. Handwashing. A servant is kneeling in front of the table with basin and towel. 2. Grace. Odo, the dominating figure at the table, easily identified by his tonsure, blesses the food. 3. Eating the meal. The Duke, sitting to the right of the Bishop, forms the transition from the previous stage and this one. With an attentive glance at Odo, he has already one hand on the dish. Three other persons, including an elderly bearded man, are eating and drinking. 4. The meal is over. A man next to Odo is clearly signifying that it is time to proceed further.

The only dining tool of those times, the knife, lies to the left of the table. In front of Bishop Odo is a fish – 29 September, the day after the invasion, was a Friday and thus a day of fasting for a cleric.

HIC COQUITUR CARO. ET HIC MINISTRAVERUNT MINISTRI. HIC FECERUNT PRANDIUM.
ET HIC EPISCOPUS CIBUM ET POTUM BENEDICIT. ODO EPISCOPUS. WILLELM. ROTBERT.
Here meat is cooked. And here the waiters serve the food. Here they made lunch. [The texts which had
hitherto been in only a single colour are from now on in several – perhaps a new and more imaginative
embroiderer for the text has taken over?] And here the Bishop blesses the food and wine. Bishop Odo.
William. Robert.

Below to the right, William is in council with his
closest collaborators, his two younger stepbrothers.
Odo and Robert Duke of Mortain. Again it appears that Odo is having his say. Robert seems to
be drawing his sword; is he impatient to take
up the fight with the English?

What can they be discussing? Perhaps the warning which according to Poitiers had been given
William by a wealthy Norman residing in England,
Robert, the son of the noble Lady Wimarc. Robert's messenger had brought the Duke the news of
King Harold's victory over both his brother Tostig
and the King of Norway, Harold Hardrada, 'who
is considered to be the greatest warrior under the
sun', and had advised William to be both wise and
cautious, to keep behind his fortifications and not
to rush into battle.

Supervised by captains, workmen start building a fort at Hastings. Two of the men start fighting and the presentation of this incident is one of the features that proves that the tapestry was produced soon after the events depicted, while they were still topical.

The fortifications consist of a stratified mound on which is placed a palisade or fence, flanked by watchtowers. The energetic people in the foreground with their almost graceful movements may be digging the moat which normally goes with such an installation.

William, in civilian dress, is receiving a messenger bringing news of King Harold's movements. Here the consecrated three-tongued banner with cross which Pope Alexander II had sent the Duke together with his approval of the 'crusade' against England is shown for the first time.

The burning of the fine tall house is probably another example of a specific event of particular importance. One of the two incendiaries has a spear while the other is unarmed and does not look warlike. He is partly bald, corpulent and stalky legged – it is almost a portrait. Two people are fleeing from the burning building: A well-dressed woman the third and last in the main tapestry frieze and a forlorn little boy whom she is leading by her wrist. 'The widow and the fatherless, symbolic of war's everlasting innocent victims', Simone Bertrand calls them.

After a fanciful representation of the town of Hastings we see Duke William, now clad in mail from top to toe, helmeted, and with his sword a his side. He is holding a lance with banner flying. A groom holds his Spanish war-horse – a gift from King Alfonso of Leon. The picture heralds a new and decisive phase in the campaign: the military struggle with the English army.

ISTE IUSSIT UT FODERETUR CASTELLUM AT HESTENGAMCEASTRA. HIC NUNTIATUM EST WILLELMO DE HAROLD(O). HIC DOMUS INCENDITUR.
HIC MILITES EXIERUNT DE HESTENGA...

He ordered defences to be dug at Hastings [The use of 'at' in place of the Latin 'ad' is cited as a sign that an Englishman has written the text. The designation for Hastings is also influenced by Anglo-Saxon usage]. Here William receives news of Harold. Here a house is set on fire. Here the soldiers left Hastings...

The Battle of the Grey Apple-Tree

When King Harold was informed of this, he gathered together a great host, and came to oppose him at the grey apple-tree, and William came upon him unexpectedly before his army was set in order...

The Anglo-Saxon Chronicle, 1066

The French cavalry leave Hastings to move north-west along the old highway leading to London. William rides at their head, holding a sceptre-like staff or club which he later wielded during the entire battle.

The riders following him in close formation are depicted in masterly fashion as they change pace from a walk to a gallop with lowered lances.

When Harold Godwinson in York received news of the Norman landing, he broke camp immediately and marched post-haste to London. William learned that Harold was advancing again from London towards Hastings and decided to confront him in a surprise attack before he could reach the town.

Before this the two had exchanged letters. The clerical messengers, as servants of God, were relatively free of risk of molestation, and so it was again a monk who reported to William one day in Hastings with the following message from King Harold:

'You have come into his land with he knows not what temerity. He recalls that King Edward at first appointed you as his heir to the kingdom of England, and he remembers that he was himself sent by the King to Normandy to give you an assurance of the succession. But he knows also that the same King, his lord, acting within his rights, bestowed on him the kingdom of England when dying. Moreover, ever since the time when blessed Augustine came to these shores it has been the unbroken custom of the English to treat deathbed bequests as inviolable. It is therefore with justice that he bids you return with you followers to your own country. Otherwise he will break the friendship and the pacts he made with you in Normandy. And he leaves the choice entirely to you.'

Duke William then ordered a certain monk from

ET VENERUNT AD PRELIUM CONTRA HAROLDUM REGE(M).
...and went to do battle against King Harold.

Fécamp to deliver this answer promptly to Harold:

'It is not with temerity nor unjustly but after deliberation and in defence of right that I have crossed the sea into this country. My lord and kinsman, King Edward, made me the heir of this kingdom even as Harold himself has testified; and he did so because among all his acquaintances he held me to be the best capable of supporting him during his life and of giving just rule to the kingdom after his death. Moreover his choice was not made without the consent of his magnates since Archbishop Stigand, Earl Godwin, Earl Leofric, and Earl Siward confirmed it, swearing in his hands that after King Edward's death they would serve me as lord.'

In order to avoid unnecessary bloodshed William finally offered 'to risk my life against his in single combat to decide whether the kingdom of England should by right be his or mine'.

Poitiers adds: 'We have been careful to record all this speech in the Duke's own words rather than our own, for we wish posterity to regard him with favour.'

Upon receipt of this lengthy reply, it is reported:

'When Harold advanced to meet the Duke's envoy and heard this message he grew pale and for a long while remained as if dumb. And when the monk had asked more than once for a reply he first said: "We march at once," and then added, "We march to battle".'

The monk once again proffered Harold the suggestion made by William of a single combat between them in place of the slaughter of two armies, but Harold exclaimed, lifting his face to heaven: 'May the Lord decide this day between William and me, and may he pronounce which of us is right.'

William now had no other choice than to do battle; his troops were determined and fully prepared for war when they left Hastings at sunrise on 14 October for the battlefield by 'the grey apple-tree'.

The figures in the tapestry's borders have not been mentioned for some time. They have variously been animals, birds and fabulous creatures, but after the scene in which Harold is offered the crown (page 58) a new ornamentation is introduced; a delicately drawn vine between two sloping bars. In the border above the previous scene, there are two representations of naked couples, in both cases with the two partners facing each other; perhaps a hastily mobilised English warrior whose wife has brought him his arms, and then – the last fond embrace. A little to the right, a donkey is grazing, while a beast of prey lurks behind the bushes. In the lower border, behind William, a falcon is hunting a hare – perhaps here again some symbolism can be detected?

In answer to William's question as to whether Vital, who had been sent out to scout, has seen Harold's army, he merely points silently backwards. We do not know anything about this knight who is named, other than that he might be the Vital who was later recorded in *the Domesday Book*, like Wadard, as holding land in England under Bishop Odo.

A Norman advance patrol has reached a hill – presumably Telham Hill (see page 101) from where they can see Harold's outposts. The foremost rider is pointing with his shield in the direction of a clump of trees. His movement with the long pointed shield reminds one that this defensive device could also be used for attack. In describing William's personal contribution during the battle Poitiers says, 'not a few felt the weight of his shield.'

From the crest of a little hill on the far side of the trees, an English lookout watches for the enemy – he looks to the south-east towards the highway to Hastings, and shades his eyes with his hand against the low morning sun. It is about 8 o'clock.

A comrade hastens back to the King; obviously agitated, he announces that the Normans are in sight. The King, on horseback, receives the intelligence with a tense attitude and expression.

Harold's mount – the only horse the tapestry shows on the English side – has a short-cropped mane in contrast to those of the French. The

strange scaly configuration of the tree behind Harold is presumably to show scars from pollarding – cutting off branches for fodder or fuel.

In the course of Friday, 13 October, Harold and his army had reached the wood north of the hill, later called Senlac Hill. The riders dismounted and all bivouacked for the night. The English had no experience of cavalry warfare so their horses were no longer used. On his way south from York and while in London, the King had mustered what fresh troops he could to reinforce his army, which had suffered severe losses at the bloody Battle of Stamford Bridge less than three weeks earlier. Earls and large farmers from all of England had joined him; though not his two brothers-in-law, Earls Edwin and Morcar, whose own forces had been weakened by their defeat at the hands of Harold Hardrada shortly before King Harold had reached them. However, two of Harold's brothers,

(HIC) WILLELM DUX INTERROGAT VITAL SI VIDISSET EXERCI(TUM) HAROLDI.

ISTE NUNTIAT HAROLDUM REGEM DE EXERCITU WILLELMI DUCIS.

(Here) Duke William asks Vital whether he has seen Harold's army.

This man informs King Harold about Duke William's army.

the Earls Gyrth and Leofwine, took part in the last great conflict. They are the only names on the English side other than that of the King to be included in the Bayeux Tapestry and in the written sources describing the battle. Certain auxiliary troops supported King Harold: 'Also the land of the Danes who were allied with them had sent substantial reinforcements'.

In the Battle of Senlac – the designation employed by Orderic Vital, which is geographically more correct than the Battle of Hastings – the English army numbered about 7,000 men. The core, perhaps 1,000 strong, consisted of 'housecarls', members of the body set up by Canute the Great. In his time they were Danish warriors, and it is likely that there were still men of Nordic descent in this elite corps, with their own strict laws, who were considered the best infantrymen in Europe. The main strength of the army was made up of the fyrd, an old constitutional body established by Alfred the Great in the second half of the 9th century. These were levied from the peasantry, and scarcely trained in the art of war

but, as Poitiers acknowledges: 'All were inspired by the love of their country which they desired, however unjustly, to defend against foreigners.'

Harold's total forces were little greater than William's, but Guillaume de Poitiers, who wishes to suggest that his master defeated a superior enemy, writes: 'If any classic poet had described Harold's host, he would have said that rivers dried up and forests became plains wherever they advanced.'

The tapestry returns to depicting the Normans in the next scenes. William's army is now preparing for battle.

Poitiers recounts that on the morning of 14 October the Duke had attended mass and partaken of the Sacrament. He then hung round his neck the relics over which Harold had sworn his broken oath. When William had donned his coat of mail he had accidentally put it on in reverse, 'but he merely laughed and did not allow the unlucky omen to disturb him'.

PREPARA ... RENSE:VI RILITER

HIC WILLELM DUX ALLOQUITUR SUIS MILITIBUS UT PREPARARENT SE VIRILITER...
Here Duke William exhorts his soldiers to prepare themselves like men...

When the troops were assembled, the Duke made a speech to them, in which he incited his men to fight, not merely for victory, but also for survival: 'There is no road for retreat. In front, your advance is blocked by an army and a hostile countryside; behind you, there is the sea where an enemy fleet bars your flight. Men who are worthy of the name do not allow themselves to be dismayed by the number of their foes. The English have again and again fallen to the sword of an enemy; often, being vanquished, they have submitted to a foreign yoke; nor have they ever been famed as soldiers. Only be bold so that nothing shall make you yield, and victory will gladden your hearts.'

Before dawn on that chilly October morning, William's army moved out of Hastings and marched north-west along the highway leading to London.

The English forces, which had taken up their positions on the ridge of Senlac Hill about 10 kilometres from Hastings, could hardly have been able to observe the enemy troops before they had passed Telham Hill a couple of kilometres away. On the north side of Telham Hill, William's army swung to the left away from the road and fanned out in battle order in three columns which together may have presented a front of 800 to 1,000 metres in width (see map on page 101). All three columns were grouped in three detachments: foremost, archers with short powerful bows; in the middle, heavier infantry clad in mail and armed with sword, spear and shield, and in the rear, cavalry likewise mailclad and armed with swords, lances, javelins and long shields.

Of the three columns, the one to the left consisted mainly of people from Brittany, led by Count Alan Fergant who was married to William's daughter Constance; the one to the right was made up of auxiliary troops from other French districts and Flanders, under Edward the Confessor's brother-in-law, Eustace of Boulogne and Roger of Montgomery; the central column was

ET SAPIENTER AD PRELIUM CONTRA ANGLORUM EXERCITUM.
...and wisely for the battle against the English army.

composed of Normans under the command of William, who had his two stepbrothers Odo and Robert as deputy commanders. The papal banner was borne before the Duke.

Senlac Hill rises 15 to 20 metres above the meadow-like terrain in front of it. The English troops were tightly massed on the ridge of the hill. Harold had chosen his fighting post in the middle, identifiable by the King's two standards: the dragon of Wessex and the 'golden warrior' which was his personal emblem. The central sector was defended mainly by the housecarls, the flanks by soldiers from the fyrd. The most important weapons of the housecarls was the terrifying long-handled 'Danish' waraxes which were said to be able to fell a man and his horse with a single blow. Swords, javelins and clubs were also part of their armament.

Charles H. Lemmon has pointed out that the tapestry's representation of the housecarl 'uniform' is not correct; they were clad almost identical to the Normans, but wore short tight-fitting leather doublets without sleeves and with iron rings sewn on, trousers with straps round the bottom and sandals on their feet. Their hair was long and their helmets, with nose-pieces like those of the Normans, had long leather flaps that fell over their shoulders. Their lime-wood shields were almost a metre long. Members of the fyrd were generally clad in leather doublets and caps. Most of them carried small circular shields and their arms consisted of spears, short axes, scythes, slings and clubs headed with stone.

'At the third hour', i.e. 9 o'clock, William advanced his forces slowly towards the ridge and the blowing of horns from each side announced that the battle had begun.

When the French archers were less than 100 metres away from the English positions they fired their arrows, but this opening attack proved ineffective. Some arrows went over the heads of Harold's men while others stuck in their long shields as shown in the tapestry.

When the archers had released their own arrows it was then customary for the enemy to gather them up and shoot them back. Thus both parties could continue this exchange for some time.

HIC CECIDERUNT LEWINE ET GYRD FRATRES HAROLDI REGIS.
Here fell Leofwine and Gyrth, brothers of King Harold
[The old English and Nordic D in the spelling of the
name Gyrd is thought to disclose an Anglo-Saxon hand].

However, the English had very few archers – only one is depicted in the tapestry. When the attackers had used what they had in their quivers, they had therefore to cease shooting until new stocks of arrows were forthcoming from their own supplies.

A second phase in the battle now began, a general infantry attack over the entire front. Poitiers relates: 'But the English resisted valiantly, and they hurled back spears and javelins and weapons of all kinds together with axes and stones fastened to pieces of wood. The shouts of the Normans and the barbarians were drowned in the clash of arms and by the cries of the dying, and for a long time the battle raged with the utmost fury…' Robert Wace mentions in *Roman de Rou* the war cries of the two parties: The French 'Diex aie!' (God help!), and the English 'Ut, ut!' (out, out!). The latter must have sounded like the baying of a pack of thousands of hounds.

Poitiers names a number of the knights taking part in the battle on the Norman side, colourful names which for the most part were to live on in English history: Roger of Montgomery (later Earl of Shrewsbury), William Fit-Osbern (Earl of Hereford), Walter Giffard, Hugo of Montford, Rodulf of Tosny, William of Warenne (Earl of Surrey). He specially mentions that 'a certain Norman, Robert, son of Roger of Beaumont, found himself that day in battle for the first time; he was as yet but a young man and he performed feats of valour worthy of perpetual remembrance. At the head of the troop which he commanded on the right wing, he attacked with the utmost bravery and success'.

William himself, who personally commanded the joint forces during the entire battle, 'excelled them all both in bravery and soldier-craft, so that one might esteem him as at least the equal of the most praised generals of ancient Greece and Rome. He was everywhere, battling fearlessly and came to the rescue of many…'

In one of the violent hand-to-hand encounters depicted with thrilling realism in the Bayeux Tapestry, one of Harold's brothers, Leofwine, was killed, and in another, his brother Gyrth.

MVL·ANGLI ET FRANCI·INPR[E]LIO

The English resistance, which had the character of a regular counterattack, was so violent that William's left flank, composed of forces from Brittany, gave way and fled in panic. Contrary to their King's orders, the members of the fyrd on Harold's right flank succumbed to the temptation to pursue the enemy down the hill-slope and on to the flat meadow to the south. This breakup of the front affected the Norman cavalry which was held in readiness for the next phase of the battle, and in the ensuing confusion William was thrown from his horse. A wild cry rumoured that the Duke had fallen; but he quickly mounted another horse and pushing back his helmet so that all about could see his face, he shouted, 'Look at me well. I am still alive and by the grace of God I shall yet prove victor!' (see the scene to the right). Morale was restored and William mustered the horsemen for a counterattack against the English pursuers. They were driven up on to a hillock where they were soon overpowered (above, centre, see also map on page 101).

If William had really been killed, or if he had not succeeded in convincing his men that he was alive, it would certainly have meant defeat for the Normans. The military historian, General J. F. C. Fuller, compares the loss of a commander-in-chief at that time with the effect it would have in a modern war if the entire general staff of an army were suddenly annihilated. All initiative and all communication would break down, and the battle would be lost. The most critical moment in the whole battle for William was when they thought he was dead. Had Harold been aware of the situation and taken advantage of it to counterattack right away, he could have made the panic complete, cut down the enemy's infantry and split his cavalry, so that the only possibility would have been to beat an instant retreat to Hastings. Harold's hesitation and William's resolute behaviour saved the Normans from defeat.

In the third phase of the battle, William sent in his cavalry in full strength. The English were by then weakened, though by no means defeated. Even by the end of the afternoon the outcome of

(HIC CECIDERUNT SIMUL) ANGLI ET FRANCI IN PRELIO. HIC ODO EPISCOPUS BACULUM TENENS
CONFORTAT PUEROS. HIC EST WILLELM DUX. E(USTA)TIUS. HIC FRANCI PUGNANT.
Here fell both the English and French simultaneously in the battle. Here Bishop Odo with
a staff in hand encourages his squires ['boys']. Here is Duke William. Eustace [of Boulogne].
Here the French do battle.

ET CECIDERUNT QUI ERANT CUM HAROLDO. HIC HAROLD REX INTERFECTUS EST.
And those who were with Harold fell. Here King Harold was killed.

the battle had not been decided. The fighters on Senlac Hill repulsed one attack after another with severe losses on both sides.

Towards evening, when both sides were almost exhausted after the long fierce struggle, William initiated the fourth phase of the battle. He again sent his archers forward, now supplied with new amply replenished quivers, which they stuck in the ground before them as seen in the tapestry. When they resumed shooting, they aimed high so that their arrows now rained down on King Harold and the core of housecarls still closely surrounding him and his banners. Their wall of shields gave no protection, and the heavy losses suffered made the final decisive cavalry assault possible.

The lower border of the Bayeux Tapestry, which from the moment the first Norman horsemen meet the English is incorporated into the battle picture, shows how the archers now aim higher than before (page 86). It also demonstrates how the valuable coats of mail were stripped from the dead and how swords and shields were collected (page 87). The artist has reproduced the fallen and mutilated with sinister realism; the men lying here are indeed dead!

Below the text HIC HAROLD REX INTERFEC-TUS EST is seen one of the King's standardbearers collapsing with his banner falling to the ground, a soldier with his spear raised ready to be thrown and the other standard-bearer follows. Behind the standard-bearer is a tall man grasping an arrow which has struck him in the forehead or eye. In the course of time, many have thought this man was Harold, but most modern researchers, e.g. Sir Frank Stenton and C. H. Gibbs-Smith, are convinced, not least because of the composition of the scene, that Harold is the figure under the conclusion of the inscription. He has been ridden down by a Norman horseman, falling like a log and letting go his long battle-axe. The French Bishop, Guy of Amiens, relates that Harold was downed by four knights: Eustace of Boulogne, a son of Count Guy of Ponthieu, Walter Giffard and Hugo of Montford.

With the death of Harold, the battle approached its close after having lasted for eight hours. In the dusk the last Englishmen still able to move were put to flight.

In the last picture of the tapestry, a small group of English civilians, several bearing clubs and one grasping an arrow which has hit him in the eye, are fleeing. Below, two riders are whipping their horses and in front a man seems to be struggling with a vine in which he is entangled – the very last scene is as much a riddle as several others have been.

Yet has this always been the last scene? The Bayeux Tapestry today is incomplete. The vertical ending of the border is missing, and many historians agree that there must have been at least one more scene – a more worthy conclusion to this historical cavalcade. Perhaps the answer lies in a poem praising William the Conqueror's daughter Adela, written round about the year 1100 by Baudri de Bourguiel, later Bishop of Dol. In this he describes some beautiful wall hangings which he imagines decorate the Princess's bedchamber. The theme in one of them corresponds in detail with the Bayeux Tapestry. He furthermore relates that each single scene is accompanied by a text. Although Adela's hanging is described as having been made of gold, silver and silk – not wool and linen – it is likely that he has actually used the Bayeux Tapestry as his model. If this is the case, his poem can give us information as to what the last scene presented: Normans occupying English towns and homage being paid to William as King!

One of the most decisive, and for that time bloodiest, battles in history was at an end. Charles H. Lemmon estimates William's fatal casualties at more than thirty percent of his total forces, and the English percentage killed to have been considerably greater.

In an apt play on words, the French have subsequently called the scene of the bloody battle at Senlac 'Sanguelac' – 'Blood Lake'. This name was used by Tennyson with dramatic effect in his play *Harold*, in which during the night before the battle the King in a dream meets Edward the Confessor, his brothers Tostig and Wulfnot and the profaned Norman saints, all of whom pronounce the ominous word 'Sanguelac'!

Poitiers recounts that when Duke William returned to the scene after the battle, 'he could not gaze without pity on the carnage, although the slain were evil men, and although it is good

ET FUGA
VERTERUNT
ANGLI
And
the English
fled.

and glorious in a just war to kill a tyrant. The bloodstained battleground was covered with the flower of the youth and nobility of England. The two brothers of the King were found near him, and Harold himself, stripped of all badges of honour, could not be identified by his face, but only by certain marks on his body.'

In *Roman de Rou*, it is related that the two monks Osgod and Ailrik, sent by their abbot in Waltham Abbey in Essex to secure the body of Harold, the benefactor of their monastery, searched in vain for it on the battlefield. When they approached the King's former mistress, Edith Swan-neck, for her assistance, she showed greater ability than the monks in finding the corpse of the man she had once loved. Heinrich Heine in his epic poem *Schlachtfeld bei Hastings* describes the macabre search and retrieval of Harold's body, which Edith recognises from three small marks on his shoulder, 'Denkmäler der Lust'.

According to Poitiers, the King's corpse was taken to the Duke's camp. William entrusted it to a certain William Malet for burial, and not to Harold's mother Gyda who had offered to pay for the body its weight in gold. It was said that he who had guarded the coast with such zeal ought to be buried there – but this was only mockery, writes Poitiers.

As far as can be judged, Harold Godwinson was laid to rest in the Holy Cross Abbey in Waltham.

IN MEMORIAM

GRENFELL.—In ever-loving memory of GEORGE BEVIL, Flying Officer, R.A.F.V.R., killed on active service, Oct. 14, 1942; also of ARTHUR WILFRED, Sec. Lieut., 60th Rifles who died of wounds received in action at Sidi Rezegh, Nov. 21, 1941, dearly loved sons of WINIFRED and the late ARTHUR GRENFELL, and stepsons of J. P. Cardiff-Watson.

HAROLD OF ENGLAND.—Killed in action defending his country from the invader, 14th October, 1066.

SWEET-ESCOTT.—In ever-living devoted memory of our only son, " BILL " (Lieut., R.F.A.), killed in action on October 14th, 1918.

For a number of years round about the jubilee in 1966, on each 14 October, the date of the Battle of Hastings, this notice appeared in the London daily The Times. Harold Godwinson is not forgotten.

Today the battlefield is an area of open land just outside the small town which is entitled to bear the name of Battle. The little mound which is shown in the Bayeux Tapestry (page 84) is still easily recognisable in the western part of the battleground. However, all traces of the most decisive battle on English soil are gone, not a bone from the fallen, not a ring from their suits of mail, not an arrowhead is preserved – the earth has caused them all to disintegrate. The picturesque Battle Abbey rises atop Senlac Hill as a monument to the victor. In the 13th-century wing of the Abbey there is now a girls' school. Where Harold's housecarls fought their last fight, till their war cries fell silent, there is now a school playing field with shrill girlish voices echoing from the ancient walls. This picture was taken from the spot where King Harold fell and where William the Conqueror had the high altar of the Abbey Church erected. The bases of the mighty columns lie like fossilised stumps of enormous trees. The grey apple-tree is long since gone but other trees cover the historic spot. Photo: M. R.

In the margin of a 13th-century manuscript is this little sketch of Battle Abbey, at that time one of the wealthiest in England. British Museum.

William I, King of England

He was crowned at last with the consent of the English or at least at the desire of their magnates.

Guillaume de Poitiers

King Harold's army was defeated, he himself was killed and with him a large proportion of England's nobility, including two of his brothers. The power of the Godwin family was broken. Duke William had won the first battle on English soil, but it was to take six years before the last was won and all of England conquered. Indeed, it was nine years before Wales also came under his dominion.

Before the battle of 'the grey apple-tree' – which must have been a well-known landmark in the area – William had vowed to God, through the Pope, to build an abbey on the battlefield when he had vanquished the usurper Harold. Shortly after his victory he fulfilled his promise and ordered the construction of an abbey on Senlac Hill itself. According to William of Jumièges, 'out of love for those from both sides who had fallen in this conflict', it was dedicated to the Holy Trinity and inhabited by monks from Marmoutier. The high altar of the Abbey Church was built on the exact spot where Harold's standard stood and where the King met his death. According to *Cronicon Monasterii de Bello* from the 12th century, William 'desired that in order to keep his triumph in continual remembrance the place might be called Battel...'

When William had recovered from the exhaustion of the battle, his first move was a punitive expedition against the inhabitants of the little town of Romney, east of Hastings, who had attacked the Norman ship or ships which had landed too far to the east, while the main force had reached the shore unmolested in Pevensey Bay (page 66).

From Romney he continued eastward to the town of Dover where the strong fortress surrendered without a fight. Here William demonstrated his sense of justice which was later stressed as one of his favourite qualities. Some of his soldiers had set fire to the fortress even though the garrison were preparing for an unconditional capitulation. The fire spread and some houses in the town were burnt down. It is reported from several quarters that William reprimanded his men in great anger, and paid compensation on the spot for the damage done.

From Dover he followed the old Roman highway towards Canterbury, but he had hardly started when he was met by a deputation from the cathedral city who gave him hostages and swore their allegiance to him. In Canterbury the Duke became seriously ill and had to postpone his further advance for a month, but not even sickness could curb his energies. From his sickbed he sent a demand to Edward the Confessor's widow, King Harold's sister Edith, for her dowager residence of Winchester, and promptly accepted the surrender of that town. His next goal was London.

In the meanwhile, however, a group of English thanes conspired to halt the victorious advance of the alien Duke and to give England one of her own countrymen as king. The monk Florence of Worcester records thus:

'On hearing of his death Earls Edwin and Morcar, who had withdrawn themselves from the conflict, went to London and sent their sister, Queen Edith (Aldgyth), to Chester. But Aldred, Archbishop of York, and the said earls, with the citizens of London and the shipmen planned to elevate to the throne Prince Edgar, grandson of Edmund Ironside, and promised to renew the contest under his command. But while many were preparing to go to the fight, the earls withdrew their assistance and returned home with their army. Meanwhile Count William was laying waste Sussex, Kent, Hampshire, Surrey, Middlesex and

Hertfordshire, burning villages and slaying their inhabitants until he came to Berkhamsted. There Archbishop Aldred, Wulfstan, Bishop of Worcester, Walter, Bishop of Hereford, Prince Edgar, the Earls Edwin and Morcar, the chief men of London and many others came to him, and giving hostages they surrendered and swore fealty to him. So he entered into a pact with them, but none the less permitted his men to burn villages and keep on pillaging. But when Christmas Day drew near, he went to London with his whole army in order that he might be made King.'

William I is crowned

Here Poitiers can supplement the terse account of the coronation given by English sources. He says that the Duke did not let himself be 'made king' at first and that the bishops and thanes actually had to implore him to take the crown. 'We are accustomed to obey a king,' they said, 'and we desire to have a king as lord.'

'...The Duke therefore took counsel with those Normans who were of proven wisdom and fidelity, and explained to them why he was reluctant to accede to the demand of the English. Whilst the country was still unsettled and so much resistance remained to be crushed, he would prefer the peace of the kingdom to its crown. Besides, if God were to accord him this honour, he would wish to be crowned with his wife... His familiar counsellors, however, although they respected his motives and his wisdom, none the less urged him to take the crown, for they knew that this was the fervent desire of his whole army.' It took a long and earnest monologue by Count Haimo of Thouars, 'who was as famous for his speech as for his strong right arm', before the Duke, 'after further consideration, yielded to their fervent wishes in the hope that after he had begun to reign, men would hesitate to rebel against him, or if they did so, would be more easily crushed'.

It was evidently extremely important for the French historian to stress that it was not merely the lust for power that drove his Duke to seize the Crown of England at so early a juncture.

On Christmas Day 1066, only about two months after his victory at the grey apple-tree, William I of England was anointed and crowned in the Church of St. Peter the Apostle – the precursor of Westminster Abbey. The ceremony was performed by Archbishop Aldred of York, 'a wise, good and eloquent man, famed for justice and for his mature prudence', as Poitiers describes him. The Archbishop asked the English who were present whether it was their will to have William crowned as their King 'and all without the least hesitation shouted their joyous assent, as if heaven had given them one will and one voice'. Then the Bishop of Coutances asked the Normans in French the same question and they manifested a similar enthusiasm.

However, the loud tumultuous shout which came from the church alarmed the soldiers, mounted and armed, on guard outside. They feared the shouts were a bad sign, and in their panic they began to set fire to the houses in the vicinity!

Inside in the dim church, Archbishop Aldred now placed the crown on William's head and led him to the throne.

Poitiers concludes his description of the solemn and dramatic event by an attempt to justify William's conquest of England and its Crown.

'This land he has gained as the legal heir with the confirmation of the oaths of the English. He took possession of his inheritance by battle. And if it be asked what was his hereditary title, let it be answered that a close kinship existed between King Edward and the son of Duke Robert whose paternal aunt, Emma, was the sister of Duke Richard II, the daughter of Duke Richard I and the mother of King Edward himself...'

In his long and detailed account of the coronation of William the Conqueror, the French writer says nothing about what the new King of England promised his subjects in return for their allegiance. However, the chronicler from Worcester does:

'Before this (since the Archbishop made it a condition), the King had sworn at the altar of

St. Peter the Apostle, and in the presence of the clergy and people, that he would defend the holy churches of God and their ministers, that he would rule justly and with kingly care the whole people placed under him, that he would make and keep right law, and that he would utterly prohibit all spoliation and unrighteous judgements…'

Danish invasion – and a doubtful death sentence

In the spring of 1067, Duchess Matilda was called to England to be crowned as the country's queen on Whitsunday. In the following year she gave birth to the first of her children to be born on English soil. He was given the name of Henry (Beauclerc) and in due course became King after his brother William Rufus, the second son.

When William the Conqueror left for England in 1066, his eldest son Robert Shorthose was about twelve years old. He was at that time formally installed as his father's successor to the dukedom but, as he was a minor, it was his mother who was Regent in her husband's absence, with the support of chosen Norman thanes. William divided his time between England and Normandy, both places needing a firm hand at the helm. Norman castles sprang up in the conquered country at all strategic places. Already at about the time of his coronation, William had started the construction of London's distinctive stronghold, the Tower. It was built of the characteristic yellowish-grey limestone from the Caen area across the Channel.

In the years immediately after the coronation, rebellion smouldered all over in England. The prosperous trading city of Exeter, where Earl Godwin's widow Gyda and Harold Godwinson's sons by Edith Swan-neck resided, refused to swear allegiance to William in 1068. The King had to besiege the city for 18 days before it surrendered. The rearguard of his army consisted of Englishmen and this was the first time that Norman and domestic troops were in action together. Gyda

Perhaps a scene like this originally concluded the Bayeux Tapestry: William I enthroned bearing the crown of England on his head. There is a striking likeness between this portrait and several of those in the tapestry. This miniature from a manuscript is from the 11th century. British Library.

and her grandchildren fled to Ireland. The following year the young sons of Harold Godwinson attempted to invade England, but were defeated by the Breton Earl of Cornwall, Brian.

The Anglo-Saxon areas in general adjusted more readily to the new rulers, while the old Scandinavian-influenced regions in the north and east showed less desire to cooperate. The brother of the Danish King Sweyn Estridsen, Asbjørn, took advantage of this when in the autumn of 1069 he assembled a fleet of 240 longships and sailed for England. He was accompanied by some of Sweyn's sons and other thanes, including Bishop Christian of Århus. After sporadic raiding and plundering in the south of England, the fleet sailed up the east coast. The Danes succeeded in capturing

York, where until that spring the castle had been commanded by the bluff William Fitz-Osbern, son of William's cousin and old grand-seneschal. They received support from their old kinsmen in the area, but when William arrived with his army they could not hold their positions. They retired to their ship and continued raiding the coast. William was obliged to bribe them to sail home.

A group of Breton barons, who had accompanied William to England and had been rewarded with grants of land, revolted against the King in 1075 while he was away in Normandy. Among the causes of their dissatisfaction was William's adoption of the Anglo-Saxon system of public justice, which gave him firmer control over them than he had ever had in Normandy. Furthermore his constant military campaigns in France may have imposed financial burdens upon them. Their leader was the half English, half Breton Earl of Norfolk, Ralph de Gael. Earl Waltheof of Huntingdon, a son of the aforementioned Siward Jarl and the husband of King William's niece Judith, was initiated into the plans and invited to join the rebels but he declined. Archbishop Lanfranc, who at the time was William's Viceroy in England, wrote to the King about the matter, but asked him to stay where he was while the Archbishop and the loyal earls put down the rebellion.

Ralph was forced to retire to the town of Norwich where he left the defence of the castle to his young wife, a daughter of William Fitz-Osbern, while he put to sea to seek aid in Denmark. Shortly afterwards, King Sweyn Estridsen's son Canute (the Holy) and a certain Earl Hakon led a warfleet of 200 ships across the sea. When they reached Norfolk, the town of Norwich had fallen and the Danes' expedition was reduced to a traditional plundering raid along the coast before it sailed away. Ralph escaped to Brittany, but other ringleaders were caught and punished.

Orderic Vital relates that the popular Earl Waltheof 'was summoned before the King and, according to evidence by his wife, accused of knowledge and complicity in the aforementioned treason and infidelity towards his sovereign. Open-ly and honestly he admitted that the traitors had entrusted him with their dastardly plan, but added that he had never consented to this nefarious undertaking…' Waltheof languished in prison in Winchester for a year before his enemies finally had him sentenced to death.

Early in the morning on the day of the execution, Waltheof knelt to say the Lord's Prayer. 'But when he had said: "Lead us not into temptation"', reports Vital, 'he broke into tears, and the executioner impatiently drew his sword and cut off the earl's head from his body with a mighty stroke. However, in the hearing of all assembled the severed head said in a loud voice: "But deliver us from evil! Amen".'

William's brutal liquidation of the last of the old Anglo-Saxon earls created a great stir in England, not least because William himself had forbidden capital punishment, even for murder. Orderic Vital doubtless expresses the thoughts in many minds when he writes: 'It is an open question whether his execution can be justified both morally and legally.' Perhaps Waltheof was removed because, being the son of a Nordic earl, he could exert a dangerous influence upon the Danish and Norwegian elements in the population and on the still militant naval power Denmark.

Ralph de Gael continued the revolt against William from Brittany, and unrest spread along the Normandy border. The Duke had constantly to be on the warpath and engaged in battles with results not always in his favour. The French King Philip I, interested in separating England and Normandy, took part in the conflict on the side of the rebels.

The hardest blow against William, however, came from his eldest son. Robert Shorthose was impatient at not being handed over the real power in Normandy, which his father did not have in mind to do until forced to by death. He joined the rebels and attempted a coup. He got so far as to besiege the castle in Rouen, but its commandant sent for aid and the attack was repulsed. *The Anglo-Saxon Chronicle* relates: 'In this year Robert fought against his father, and wounded him in the hand; and his horse was killed under him;

Robert Shorthose, William the Conqueror's eldest son, was almost constantly in opposition to his father, who however forgave him on his deathbed and acknowledged him as Duke of Normandy. Robert never became King of England; the third brother William Rufus succeeded his father in 1087. An elder brother Richard had died 10 years before. Robert joined the Crusades in 1096 and distinguished himself in battle against the Saracens but declined to be made King of Jerusalem. During his absence William Rufus died and Henry Beauclerc became King. After his return, Robert tried unsuccessfully to seize the crown of England. He was taken prisoner during a battle in 1106, and confined in Cardiff Castle where he died after 28 years of imprisonment. His beautiful monument in Gloucester Cathedral shows him as a crusader at rest with his ducal crown on his mail-clad head. Royal Commission on Historical Monuments, Crown Copyright.

and he who brought up another for him was immediately killed by a bolt from a crossbow, and many there were slain or taken prisoner; and Robert returned to Flanders. We do not wish, however, to chronicle here more of the harm which he (did to) his father…'

England under Norman rule

William the Conqueror's last years were embittered by continuous conflicts, by illness and a growing apprehension that his death would mean disharmony and rivalry amongst his sons and the thanes of the realm. The best features in the old English law had been retained, at least formally. In William's own scanty legislation, his decree on the separation of clerical and secular jurisdiction in the Courts of the Hundred was of great significance. A new style and method of building left its stamp on English towns in the course of the years. The Norman rule gave the English language many loan words from French, particularly as regards governmental, legislative and administrative matters. French influence also

came to affect culture, literature and architecture. With French being the court language for a century and a half, it was spoken by the upper class, but very few French words were adopted in agriculture and fishing.

William the Conqueror was a statesman of very great stature and strong personality, for better and for worse. His legendary avarice was already apparent soon after his victory in 1066. All property owned by his opponents was confiscated. Large tracts of land were, as promised, given to the Frenchmen who had supported him. In many cases, the widows and children of men who had fallen at Senlac had to buy their own land back from the King at outrageous prices. His tax levies were a constant source of complaint. After his coronation, when William returned to Normandy, even the magnates in this prosperous French duchy were dumbfounded at the sight of the enormous quantities of gold, silver and other English valuables that the King could display.

Early in the 12th century, William of Malmesbury characterised the habits and way of life of both the native English and the Norman newcomers in the period just after the Conquest. He writes about his compatriots thus:

'Drinking in parties was a universal custom, in which occupation they passed entire days and nights. They consumed their whole fortune in mean and despicable houses, unlike the Normans and the French who in noble and splendid mansions live with frugality. The vices attendant upon drunkenness followed in due course and these, as is well known, enervate the human mind. Hence it came about that they engaged William more with rashness and fury than with military skill, and so they doomed themselves and their country to slavery by giving him an easy victory in a single battle... They were wont to eat until they became surfeited and to drink until they were sick. These latter qualities they imparted to their conquerors; as to the rest they adopted their manners.'

After admitting that he did not wish to generalise and that he knew that many Englishmen of all stations in life were nevertheless god-fearing, William then described the Normans with a blend of praise and blame: 'They were at that time, as they are now, exceedingly particular in their dress, and delicate in their food, but not to excess. They are a race inured to war, and can hardly live without it, fierce in attacking their enemies, and when force fails, ready to use guile or to corrupt by bribery... They are faithful to their lords though slight offence gives them an excuse for treachery. They weigh treason by its chance of success, and change their opinions for money. They are the most polite of people...'

Not all the Normans who came to England felt at home there; some returned voluntarily, others were forced to do so, but new adventurers left Normandy and crossed the Channel to try their luck in the conquered country. Intermarriage between the two peoples helped to level out differences. However, there is still talk, especially among foreigners, about 'characteristic' Anglo-Saxon or Norman traits in the English people whose heritage after all derives from the Celts, Romans, Danes and Norwegians.

The English themselves do not favour such differentiation. Today they are conscious of belonging to a single nation, and have all doubtless come to terms with the Norman Conquest of nine hundred years ago. Perhaps some even feel as the historian Thomas Carlyle did in 1858 when he expressed his view of the English people thus: 'Without the Normans what had it ever been? A gluttonous race of Jutes and Angles capable of no great combinations; lumbering about in pot-bellied equanimity; not dreaming of heroic toil and silence and endurance, such as lead to the high places of the Universe, and the golden mountain tops where dwell the spirit of the Dawn.'

The author Daniel Defoe in his poem *The True-Born Englishman* from 1701 speculates how one can be 'A *True-Born Englishman* of *Norman Race?*' and concludes:

Conquest, as by the Modern 'tis exprest,
May give a Title to the Lands possest:
But that the Longest Sword shou'd be so Civil,
To make a *Frenchman English,* that's the Devil.

William the Conquerors posthumous reputation

In 1083 Queen Matilda died in Caen and was buried in her own Abbaye-des-Dames. She had been a good and faithful wife to her husband and the only shadow cast upon their marriage, so it is said, was that she had been over-indulgent with her extravagant and improvident first-born son Robert, and advanced him money from his father's treasury.

William died four years later. He was now over 60. He had become stout in his later years and an old rheumatic complaint troubled him. Late in the summer of 1087 he was confined to bed with intense pain after a riding accident. For some weeks he bore the last hard trials bravely before breathing his last on 9 September in the monastery of St. Gervais, outside Rouen to the tolling of the large Cathedral bells, after having committed his soul to the Mother of God and her son, Jesus Christ.

The Anglo-Saxon Chronicle describes the terrible year when William died thus:

"One thousand and eighty-seven years after the nativity of our Lord Jesus Christ, in the twenty-first year of William's rule and reign over England, as God had granted to him, there was a very disastrous and pestilential year in this land. Such a malady fell upon men that very nearly every other person was in the sorriest plight and down with fever; it was so malignant that many died from the disease. Thereafter, in consequence of the great storms which came as we have already told, there came a great famine over all England, so that many hundreds died miserable deaths because of it…

Also in the same year, before the Assumption of St. Mary (15 August), King William went from Normandy into France with levies, and made war against his own lord, Philip the King, and slew a great number of his men, and burnt down the town of Mantes and all the holy churches inside the town. Two holy men who served God living in an anchorite's cell were there burnt to death.

After these events, King William returned again to Normandy. A cruel deed he had done, but a crueller fate befell him. How crueller? He fell sick and suffered terribly.

What can I say? That bitter death that spares neither high nor low seized him. He died in Normandy on the day following the Nativity of St. Mary. Alas! how deceitful and transitory is the prosperity of this world. He who was once a mighty king and lord of many a land, was left of all the land with nothing save seven feet of ground; and he who was once decked with gold and jewels, lay then covered with the earth…

If anyone desires to know what kind of man he was or in what honour he was held or how many lands he was lord over, then shall we write of him as we have known him, who have ourselves seen him and at one time dwelt in his court. King William, of whom we speak, was a man of great wisdom and power, and surpassed in honour and strength all those who had gone before him. Though stern beyond measure to those who opposed his will, he was kind to those

The image of the sovereign on coins
of those times should be regarded as symbolic
rather than as actual portraiture.
Judging from that of William the Conqueror,
the King has successfully adopted
the English style of moustache.
Twice actual size.

good men who loved God. On the very spot where God granted him the conquest of England he caused a great abbey to be built; and settled monks in it and richly endowed it. During his reign was built the great cathedral at Canterbury, and many another throughout all England… Among other things we must not forget the good order he kept in the land, so that a man of any substance could travel unmolested throughout the country with his bosom full of gold. No man dared to slay another, no matter what evil the other might have done him. If a man lay with a woman against her will, he was forthwith condemned to forfeit those members with which he had disported himself.

He ruled over England, and by his foresight it was surveyed so carefully that there was not a hide of land in England of which he did not know who held it and how much it was worth; and these particulars he set down in his survey.

Assuredly in his time men suffered grievous oppression and manifold injuries.

He caused castles to be built
Which were a sore burden to the poor.
A hard man was the king
And took from his subjects many marks
In gold and many more pounds in silver.
These sums he took by weight from his people,

Most unjustly and for little need.
He was sunk in greed
And utterly given up to avarice.
He set apart a vast deer preserve and imposed laws
concerning it.
Whoever slew a hart or a hind
Was to be blinded.
He forbade the killing of boars
Even as the killing of harts.
For he loved the stags as dearly
As though he had been their father…

The last lines of this poetic jeremiad refer to the gigantic game reserve that King William established in Hampshire facing the Isle of Wight, which is still called the 'New Forest'. He afforested nearly 70,000 acres of wasteland and added 14,000 acres of farmland with more than twenty villages. Primarily to prevent poaching, he forcibly moved 500 families comprising about 2,000 persons.

'He was carried alongside burning houses…'

French sources (Orderic Vital) describe the dramatic events surrounding King William's death and interment in greater detail, as might be expected:

"When the physician-in-ordinary and the others present, who had been keeping a night-long vigil while his sleep had been tranquil and not broken by either moans or sighs, perceived that he had passed away so suddenly and unexpectedly, they were filled with consternation and were beside themselves. The wealthiest among them, however, mounted their horses and left in haste to protect their property. But when the poorer retainers saw that their masters had gone away, they stole the weapons, vessels, clothing, linen and all the royal furniture and ran away, leaving the king's body almost naked on the floor of the house…"

'The rumour of the king's passing spread like wildfire and filled all hearts with joy or sorrow', continues Vital, and then reports the inexplicable arrival that very same day of the news of William's death to Norman exiles living in Rome and in Calabria!

There was great confusion in Rouen. 'Everyone left where he was to ask his wife, or whichever of his friends he met, for advice as to what he should do. Everyone removed, or decided to remove, any valuables he possessed, and hid them for fear of their being found.

At last devout men, both clerics and monks, collected their wits and their strength to form a procession and headed for St. Gervais in their ceremonial vestments, bearing cross and censers, to perform the holy Christian rite of committing the King's soul to God. Thereafter Archbishop William of Rouen ordered that his body be taken to Caen…'

After the King's bier had arrived in that town by ship and was about to be taken to its resting place, to the consternation of everyone, a fierce fire broke out in a house along the route and the conflagration spread with immense speed. Both clerics and laymen in the multitudinous following rushed about extinguishing the flames. Only the monks remained by their dead sovereign and 'he was carried alongside burning houses to the church by terrified men'.

William the Conquerors tomb has been opened twice, once during the Renaissance and once in the French revolution. On the latter occasion any remains that were left were removed. Today the coffin is empty.

Yet if there are no longer traces of King William's mortal remains, and if the pompous monument erected in the 19th century in his native town of Falaise is not a historical portrait, nevertheless there still exists one memento which bears convincing witness to the deeds of this remarkable prince who was great in everything he undertook, both for good and for evil: that long and narrow strip of linen in Bayeux.

Bibliography

Published source materials and translations

1. *The Anglo-Saxon Chronicle*, translated and published by G. N. Garmonsway, London 1960.
2. Guillaume de Poitiers: *Vie de Guillaume le Conquérant* Detailed contemporary account covering the period 1047-68. Commentated French translation of *Gesta Normannorum Ducum*. Paris 1826. Detailed English summary, see number 16 of this list.
3. Guillaume de Jumièges: *Histoire des Normands*. Brief historical account attributed to William the Conqueror written shortly after 1066. Paris 1826.
4. Adam of Bremen: *Gesta Hammaburgensis ecclesiae pontificum* (written about 1075). Translated into English by F. J. Ischan: *History of the archbishops of Hamburg-Bremen*, 1959.
5. William of Malmesbury: *De gestis regum anglorum*. A history of Kings of England written in the early 12th century. English summary, see number 16 of this list.
6. Orderic Vital (Ordericus Vitalis): *The Ecclesiastical History of England and Normandy*. Vivid accounts partly based on Poitiers. Written c. 1120-40. Edited and translated by Marjorie Chibnall, 1969-1980 from *Historia ecclesiastica*, volume 1.
7. Robert Wace: *Roman de Rou et des ducs de Normandie*. Poem in Old French from c. 1160 in which there is an account of the Battle of Hastings, but of doubtful source value. Heilbronn 1877-79.
8. Saxo: *Gesta Danorum* (Chronicle of Denmark). Written c. 1200. Several translations and editions.
9. Snorre Sturlasson: *Harold Haardraades Saga*. Written c. 1220-30.
10. Snorre Sturlasson: *Saga of Magnus the Good*. Written c. 1220-30.

Modern surveys and biographies

11. C. N. Barclay: *Battle 1066*. A brief survey of the Battle of Hastings with map and guide to the battlefield. London 1966.
12. Frank Barlow: *Edward the Confessor*. Comprehensive biography by a modern historian. London 1970.
13. Simone Bertrand: *La Tapisserie de Bayeux et la manière de vivre au onzième siecle*. An introduction to the production technique and history of the tapestry, etc. Complete reproduction of the hanging in monochrome photogravure. Bayeux 1966.
14. C. T. Chevallier (editor): *The Norman Conquest: its setting and impact*. Four valuable essays by D. Whitelock, D. C. Douglas, C. H. Lemmon and F. Barlow. London 1966.

15. David C. Douglas: *William the Conqueror*. A modern historian's analysis of the times of William the Conqueror and his actions. Many references to sources. London 1964.
16. David C. Douglas and George W. Greenaway (editor): *English Historical Documents* 1042-1189. Excerpts from, inter alia, A *monk from Caen* and *Florence of Worcester* and from Nos. 1, 2, et 5. London 1968.
17. J. E C . Fuller: *The decisive Battles of the Western World*. Includes a military analysis of the Battle of Hastings. Vol. 1, London 1965.
18. Sten Körner: *The Battle of Hastings, England and Europe, 1035-1066*. Swedish doctoral thesis dealing especially with criticism of sources. Lund 1964.
19. P. Lauer: *Le Poème de Baudri de Bourgueil adressé à Adèle... et la date de la Tapisserie de Bayeux*. Deals with a manuscript from about 1100 in the Vatican library which apparently describes the Bayeux Tapestry in *Mélanges d'Histoire offerts à M. Ch. Brémont*. Paris 1913.
20. H. R. Loyn: *The Norman Conquest*. Critical historical survey of Norman-English relations in the 11th and 12th centuries. London 1967.
21. Frank Stenton (editor): *The Bayeux Tapestry*, a comprehensive survey. An outstanding work in which a team of specialists – Sir Frank Stenton, Francis Wormald, George Wingfield Digby, Sir James Mann, John L. Nevinson, R. Allen Brown, Simone Bertrand and Charles H. Gibbs-Smith – deals with almost every topic connected with the tapestry. London 1965.
22. David M. Wilson: *The Bayeux Tapestry*. A comprehensive survey with magnificent half-size reproductions of the tapestry in colours. London 1985.
23. Wolfgang Grape: *The Bayeux Tapestry*. Has excellent reproductions of the entire tapestry; the author suggests that the tapestry was made in Normandy. Also French and German editions. Munich 1994.

Fiction

24. Heinrich Heine: *Schlachtfeld bei Hastings*. An epic poem about the search for and retrieval of King Harold's body. In the collection *Romanzero*, 1851.
25. Hope Muntz: *The Golden Warrior*. A historical novel about King Harold, told with great knowledgeability and insight. London 1948.
26. Alfred Tennyson: *Harold*. A historical drama on the life and death of Harold Godwinson, written in 1876.

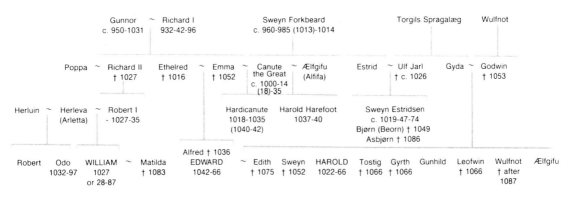

Relationship of the three main characters in the Bayeux Tapestry: William the Conqueror, Edward the Confessor and Harold Godwinson. Where three dates are given, the middle one indicates the first year on the throne while dates in parenthesis indicate the first year on the English throne.

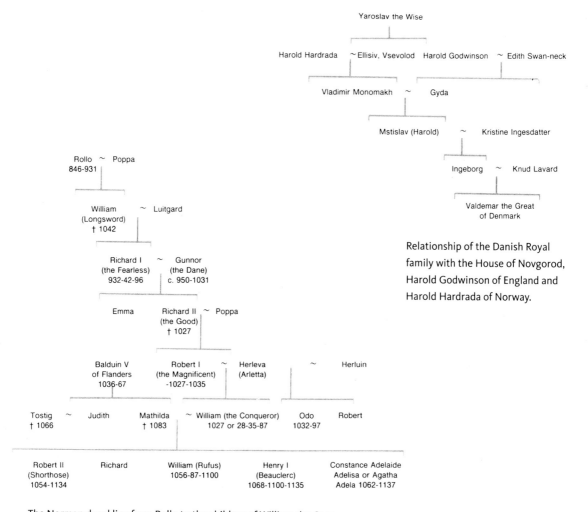

Relationship of the Danish Royal family with the House of Novgorod, Harold Godwinson of England and Harold Hardrada of Norway.

The Norman ducal line from Rollo to the children of William the Conqueror.

South England and Northwest France. The most important areas and locations mentioned in the book are shown.

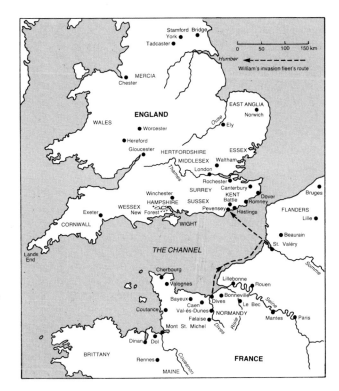

Present-day sketch showing William the Conquerors army facing Harold Godwinson's on Senlac Hill.

A: Breton Forces under Alan of Brittany

B: The Normans, directly under William the Conqueror

C: Flemish and French allies under Eustace of Boulogne and Roger of Montgomery.

"William's observation post" – at the western side of the road towards Hastings and immediately south of the railway – is behind an easily recognised petrol station.

"The Grey Apple-Tree", rallying point for Harold's army, is supposed to have been on Caldbec Hill on the northern outskirts of the present town of Battle.

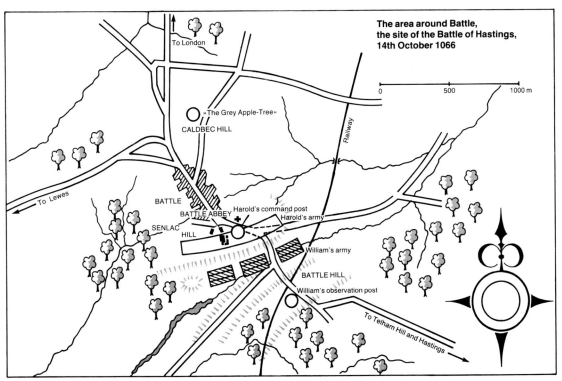

Index

Names

Subject-index